VESSEL *of* PEACE

VESSEL *of* PEACE

A Guide for Pilgrims of the Spirit

ELLEN STEPHEN
DOUG SHADEL

FOREWORD BY M. SCOTT PECK, M.D.
AUTHOR OF *THE ROAD LESS TRAVELED*

ABINGDON PRESS
Nashville

DISCARD

VESSEL OF PEACE
A GUIDE FOR PILGRIMS OF THE SPIRIT

Copyright © 2007 by Abingdon Press

All rights reserved.

This book is printed on acid-free paper.

Library of Congress Cataloging-in-Publication Data

Stephen, Ellen, 1930-
  Vessel of peace : a guide for pilgrims of the spirit / by Ellen Stephen and Doug Shadel.
    p. cm.
  ISBN 978-0-687-64255-7 (binding: pbk.,adhesive lay-flat : alk. paper)
  1. Spiritual life—Christianity. 2. God—Love. I. Shadel, Doug, 1957- II. Title.
  BV4501.3.S744 2007
  248.4—dc22
                                                                                          2007006413

07 08 09 10 11 12 13 14 15 16—10 9 8 7 6 5 4 3 2 1
MANUFACTURED IN THE UNITED STATES OF AMERICA

Contents

Contents

Foreword

There is but one Secret, and its name is God.
A few years ago I attempted to sum up my work in *The Road Less Traveled and Beyond*. It was a most prosaic attempt, save for the final chapter, entitled "The Poetry of God." Following a chapter on "The Science of God," it seemed to me appropriate to end with a format that did greater emotional justice to the subject. So I concluded the book with a twenty-page love poem to God. The last words of the poem were: In the meantime / Thank you for letting me know / That it is you / Who are the name of the game.

There are a million translations for the name of God. Some thousands of them are subsumed under the statement: "You are a part of God." The proclamation is often subject to mistranslation. In this book, however, it is spoken truthfully in the concept that we are "co-creators" with God.

We cannot create ourselves any more than we can create an iris or a simple rose petal. We are creatures—meaning that God is our original and ongoing Creator. What we can do, however, is to cooperate with God in the process of our ongoing creation. Sometimes in our youth this cooperation is unconscious. But for its fullest extent, it is required that we become conscious: conscious of God; conscious of our personal relationship with him or her; conscious of our souls; conscious of how we may interfere with God's deepest desire for our unique destinies. Such consciousness comes only with adulthood.

If it comes at all. Most largely ignore God. Many others run away from him. This is understandable. As the author of the Epistle to the Hebrews said, "It is a fearful thing to fall into the hands of the living God."

Still, it must be done if we are to become whole. We must become prayerful creatures to be fully effective co-creators. Indeed, we must have a burning thirst for glory. Yet at the very same time we must empty ourselves of any notion that glory is ours to achieve. All glory belongs to God; as co-creators the most we can hope for is to participate in it.

But that's the name of the game. In this wise book, Doug Shadel and Ellen Stephen have a great deal to teach us about how to play that game.

—*M. Scott Peck, M.D.*

Acknowledgments

Ad Majorem Dei Gloriam

With thanks to family and community for their love and support; to our especially insightful and cooperative editors at Abingdon Press; and to the wise guides and friends who have gone before and beside us on the road that leads to life.

Introduction

This is a book about spiritual freedom. Many people do not feel free. As human beings we feel bound up and filled to the brim with ideas and expectations that have been given to us by our families, peers, and culture. Some of these concepts are helpful, but many of them are hindrances to our being who we really are. Some of the most unhelpful drive us to shape ourselves to other people's ideas of what we should or ought to be.

Much of the conventional lore that we inherit is a hindrance because it is not true. Much of it is born of generalities, lazy thinking, and stereotypes. In this book we call such constructs "myths"—fictions that are passed down to us masquerading as reality. We take them on in order to win acceptance, love, and peace.

We use the metaphor of a vessel—a container—that will hold whatever is poured into it. We need a vessel that can be emptied of what is unwanted in order for it to hold what we truly desire. The human soul is such a vessel or container: it may be said that the soul is the capacity for infinite reality to be held finitely.

In his letter to the church in Philippi, Saint Paul tells us that Jesus "emptied himself, taking the form of a slave, being born in human likeness." Jesus not only emptied himself of all the perquisites of divinity, but even of human success, control, riches, status, and power. He emptied himself in order to be a vessel filled to overflowing with compassion, wisdom, and the Holy Spirit of God who is Love.

Thus, the goal is to empty oneself—the vessel—of the cultural material that is filling it in order to become spirit- or peace-filled. Here, we concentrate on seven cultural myths—seven myths that impact us negatively and can effectively block us from living our authentic lives. We seek to provide some rationale for reconnecting with truth in an age of these myths and lies. We see three primary sources of psychological "fullness" that are the ground out of which our stress and restlessness grow: beliefs from our family systems, beliefs from our peer groups, and beliefs from our culture. The point of discussing these sources of stress is to surface them and their origins into awareness. This can help us realize that the beliefs that we embody and which in many cases drive our behavior can be selected and deselected, but only if we are *aware* of them. Beliefs we hold about the world are not necessarily the same as fundamental truths.

We are made in the image of God—vessels to be filled with divine love and peace. Since, however, we have in the past been filled with misleading concepts and desires, we must consciously ally ourselves with God's grace to be reshaped into images of our true selves. We are not yet the vessels we are called to be. The prophet Jeremiah writes: "I went down to the potter's house, and there he was working at his wheel. The vessel he was making of clay was spoiled in the potter's hand, and he reworked it into another vessel, as seemed good to him." We are called to be co-shapers with God of our true capacity for love and service.

It is a paradox. Philosophers throughout the ages have said that in order to fill up with life, one must die. To experience that which is new, one must remove that which is old. If you want a more peaceful life, you can have it. But you must be intentional about making room for that new life by giving up the things that prevent you from experiencing it.

We have written this book for others who are seeking to exchange burdensome and unreal expectations for true fulfillment. Saint Ireneus said, "The glory of God is a human being fully alive." To be fully alive we strive to empty ourselves of what is no longer useful and open ourselves to the Holy Spirit of truth who will fill our minds and hearts and make us free.

SECTION 1

The Myths

CHAPTER ONE

The Myth of Perfection

Myth: The goal of human life is to continuously improve oneself in an ongoing attempt to become the best in one's field of chosen endeavor and, ultimately, achieve perfection.

Truth: The goal of life is not to become perfect as in flaw-less—it is to become ripe as in complete in every detail. To this end, we must try to empty ourselves of anything that stands in the way of accepting ourselves *as we are* and becoming aware of what God is calling us to do with our lives.

I magine for a moment that when you were born, you were like a bowl that was empty. No one had yet told you how to have good table manners or how noisy or quiet to be around adults or what kind of jeans were cool and what kind were not or that it was impolite to burp in public. In your innermost being, free from all social inputs at the beginning of life, all behavior was acceptable because it was a natural and authentic reflection of you as a human.

Then one day, minding your own business at the dinner table, you spilled your milk. Suddenly, the giant humans in the room became practically unglued and started to yell at you for creating such a mess. Your mom might even have said something like "Good little children don't spill their milk." In response to this, you stopped the action that was unacceptable to others, and you made a record of the transaction in your mind.

We are continually "filled" with notions about how we should or should not be or how perfect or imperfect we are. We are also filled with the agendas of others. The people who provide us with this input have their own beliefs and values that have been formed by their upbringing, and consequently they are passing on to us their view of the world: how much money constitutes success; how many kids constitute the perfect-sized family; how much education is enough; what kind of school our kids should go to, on and on. It is the nature of the belief systems of others and how much of those systems we allow into our "vessel" that determines our sense of self. In this chapter, we will discuss the myth that there is such a thing as "perfection" and that human beings are capable of achieving it.

Family Systems and the Myth of Perfection

We all share in the fact that the family is a primary source of data about how we should live in the world. The most important thing we learn about the myth of perfection from our family is that such a thing exists. We are led to believe that the goal of life is to continually improve, to get better, to hone our skills and our personalities so that eventually we can be at maximum effectiveness in our personal and professional life.

This belief can be reinforced at almost every turn. A child might come home with a B on a report card, and Mom says, "That's good, honey, but if you try harder, I'm sure you can get an A next time." In high school, the teenager could score ten points in the basketball game, but the coach says the next day, "That's great, but if you practice harder, I'm sure you can score twenty points per game." The adult with a job that pays well might hear the boss say, "If you work harder and hone your skills, some-day you'll make much more—maybe double."

The assumption underlying this kind of thinking is "You are not good enough where you are right now." As an example, imagine the following exchange: Parent: "Johnny isn't doing as good a job as he is capable of." Response: "Of course he is doing as good as he can. If he could do better, he would do better!" Parent: "No, you don't understand what I mean. I think Johnny has much more potential than he is showing. He can do better."

The point of this illustration is that "Johnny" may have the *potential* to do better, but the way he is *right now* is as good as he can do or he would be doing better right now. The response is correct. People are doing the best they can right now. But from the beginning of one's existence, most family systems encourage the child to "develop skills" or "improve." We are taught how to set goals and are encouraged to find role models and mentors whom we can use as a standard for our own growth and development.

And while there is nothing inherently wrong with wanting to improve or setting goals or relying on family members for input, the struggle is that some input is healthier than others. Many healthy families accept and support their members, and others use the myth of perfection as a weapon against each other. Once the perfection myth is installed, the individual can and often does use it against himself or herself, engaging in brutal self-blame and self-judgment.

Alice Miller writes how a phenomenon like this takes root in *For Your Own Good*, a book which chronicles two hundred years of German child-rearing manuals that teach parents to "break the will of the child" as a central strategy for child-rearing. Miller suggests that this technique leads to an ensuing generation of parents so full of self-loathing and devoid of self-confidence that they seek to recoup their sense of self-worth that was taken from them by their parents by breaking the will of *their* children. And so it becomes a vicious cycle.

The same cycle can exist with parents who carry the perfection myth into the relationship with their children; they seek to make up for their own imperfection by projecting impossible-to-achieve perfection standards onto their offspring. Thus we see the forty-year-old, balding, overweight father who, cut from his own high school team, demands impossible feats of athletic accomplishment from his equally average twelve-year-old son on the basketball court.

Much of this judging and demand for perfection is more about the pathology of the judger than it is a clear, objective statement about the person being judged. In the 1996 movie *Mother*, starring Albert Brooks and Debbie Reynolds, Brooks plays a forty-year-old, newly divorced science-fiction writer who is going through a midlife crisis. In his search for answers, he decides to move in with his mother to reflect on his life. The more he interacts with her, the more he is reminded of the fact that his mother is highly critical of everything he does, but especially about his being a writer.

As the son moves back into his old room, he discovers one night some old hatboxes in his closet that contain dusty manuscripts. He begins to look through them and finds that his mother wrote them before he was born. In the end, both he and his mother realize that the reason she was so critical of him and of his writing is that she had started out on her own career as a writer but had to abandon such dreams once she got pregnant. She spent the ensuing forty years unconsciously blaming her son for having to give up the one thing she felt truly passionate about. Her blame of him had nothing to do with him and everything to do with her, but because she hid (or was herself unaware of) this underlying motivation, her son grew up thinking he was inherently flawed. As Carl Jung is often quoted: "Nothing affects the environment of a child as much as the unlived life of a parent."

This realization about the root cause of her judging him sets them both free. The son realizes it is her issue that causes her to judge him, not anything he had done, and the mother realizes a painful reality she had been carrying around unconsciously for decades. Once the damaging belief surfaces, they both are freed from it.

This is an example of the power of awareness, of becoming conscious of the forces at work within our lives. Awareness carries with it the potential to free us from beliefs that hold us back, for it is only possible to empty damaging beliefs if we are first able to surface them into awareness.

For many of us, such insights do not come quickly or easily and sometimes they never surface at all. Our role models highly influence us when we are children and many times we find it difficult not to internalize such criticism from them. Once criticism is internalized, we begin to believe that we are not good enough and we need to improve.

When people are feeling particularly imperfect, when they compare themselves to others and feel like they are nowhere near as good at something, they tend to respond to others with judgment and hostility. People will pull others down to build themselves up. Conversely, when people are feeling good about themselves, usually when they have done something they are proud of, they tend to be more forgiving or accepting of others.

Over the years numerous studies have been conducted of patients in group therapy sessions. Carl Rogers and his associates at the Chicago Institute for Mental Health conducted some of the earliest studies about what kind of a therapeutic environment is most conducive to improving the self-esteem of the patient. Rogers and others hypothesized that the optimal therapeutic environment is one that has three characteristics: unconditional positive regard, empathy, and congruence (alignment between feelings and actions).

The idea is that therapy groups with these characteristics allow people to drop their social masks and begin to see and accept their authentic selves. Rogers found consistently that when exposed to such an environment, a significant number of participants reported dramatic improvement in their self-image. The implication is that by allowing the patient to empty out negative programming like the idea that perfection is achievable, patients begin to accept themselves *as they are*.

This suggests that the stimuli that we are exposed to in our normal environment, such as perfection images, cause us to be much harder on ourselves than is justified by reality. Once people experience an environment of unconditional acceptance and authentic sharing, they begin to see that others have problems just like they do but rarely if ever share those problems. In light of such authentic sharing, they realize they are not as bad as they had thought.

Peer Groups and the Myth of Perfection

If family systems plant the perfection myth seed into us as individuals, peer groups often add fertilizer and water on that seed. In peer group

8

settings, the myth of perfection is in full play, especially among teenagers, and often to the detriment of all concerned. Numerous studies show that when kids enter first grade, a majority of them actually have a positive self-image. But, by the time they are juniors in high school, the statistics are reversed, with a majority of teenagers having a negative self-image. Why?

One reason is the complicated interplay among kids whose family systems have filled them up with harsh judgment and a sense that who they are deep inside isn't good enough. These kids, filled with judgment and anger, are going to go to school with that harsh judgment spilling over onto other kids. Even those who come from accepting homes will be vulnerable to such criticism since peer influence is so powerful that even the strongest, most secure child finds it difficult not to be impacted.

A key dynamic within the peer pressure system is competition. We may measure our progress toward perfection on a kind of social bell curve in which we are constantly assessing who is ahead of us and who is behind us. Both groups are a threat to our sense of self-acceptance. Only those who are far behind us pose no threat. It is around such people that we can feel a sense of acceptance and peace.

An excellent illustration took place on a fifth-grade class field trip. There were about fifty kids on this field trip, including Kevin, a quadriplegic.

As the other kids played football and volleyball on the beach, they would engage in the back and forth about "I'm faster than you" or "You can't throw a football half as far as me." But when the kids interacted with Kevin, they were different. He was so totally nonthreatening to them that many kids gravitated toward him. It was almost as though an invisible field of unconditional love and acceptance surrounded him. Kids would joke and play with him and volunteer to help him eat lunch, but always with a kind of respect they rarely showed for one another. Their behavior changed when they were around Kevin.

He was not a threat to anyone, he was not someone who would tease others, he couldn't beat anyone in a race. His total vulnerability made him unconditionally accepting of anyone whom he encountered. And the kids responded in kind with unconditional acceptance of him. Kevin helped the kids empty themselves of their limiting beliefs about perfection and competition to find their compassionate center.

Culture and the Myth of Perfection

A strong force that teaches us the myth of perfection is the culture itself and the culture's messenger—the media. One of the key aspects of American culture is the idea of continuous improvement. The assumption underlying this idea is that who you are right now is not good enough. If who you are was good enough, you wouldn't need to improve, right?

The marketplace is filled with messages that reinforce this idea. Sports heroes and business tycoons as well as movie stars, celebrities, and models are all placed before the public by the media because they are uniquely "good" at something and ostensibly because they have maximized their potential.

Other perfection images abound: the ultimate in baseball is to pitch a "perfect" game; it is possible to bowl a "perfect" game; some opera singers are said to have "perfect" pitch; the most expensive diamonds are the ones that are "flawless"; it is possible to get a "perfect" score of 1600 on college entrance exams.

Self-improvement books, tapes, and CDs that are designed to help you "maximize your boundless potential" or "double your income" fill bookstores. We live in a kind of self-improvement, self-help Mecca where the land of opportunity has become the land of "You're doing okay, but if you buy my product, you'll do even better."

Thus, we see famous athletes endorsing athletic shoes and convincing everyone from poor inner-city youth to wealthy suburbanites to pay exorbitant prices for them. The genius of shoe companies is to see that while there are only a handful of top athletes who come close to so-called perfection, there are literally millions who want to attain it. Since they have not been given these kinds of gifts, the customers buy these shoes in order to become, in effect, vicariously perfect. The logic is, "If I can't be in the NBA (or NFL or MLB or . . .), I can at least buy shoes from someone who is."

The female image of perfection in modern culture is embodied by the supermodel and/or actress. Body image, in particular, characterizes the concept of perfection, and it is once again driven by advertisers who understand that sex appeal and beauty sells. The effect on individuals' beliefs and values, beyond convincing us to buy stuff, is that we also must look like these models of perfection. Since most of us do not look like these models and never will, we are *playing a game we cannot possibly win*. How many stories have we heard of young girls, who in a desperate attempt to gain approval from others, enter the dark world of bulimia or anorexia in order to obtain the perfect figure as modeled by Madison Avenue?

In conjunction with this pursuit of the body of perfection, there is a multibillion-dollar plastic surgery and cosmetics industry and, for men, a burgeoning industry in hair transplants and hair-growing products, all designed to inch us closer to becoming perfect-looking human beings.

And woe to the person who chooses to remain satisfied with the way he or she is. We have come to equate standing pat with losing, and losing in our culture is the ultimate source of self-judgment and self-blame. Many people believe there is no such thing as standing still because you are either moving ahead or falling behind.

But the myth of perfection is not limited to appearance. Because of the pervasiveness of advertising imagery and the focus on success, Americans hold specific beliefs, conscious or unconscious, about the whole of their lives. We are constantly assessing where we are in relationship to others, all the while using images we see on everything from billboards to television as the barometer of our career success *and* our core identity.

We can watch a television program profiling highly successful entrepreneurs and immediately want to know the people's ages, where they came from, and what advantages or disadvantages they had growing up in order to compare ourselves to them. In addition, we might constantly compare ourselves to people we work with, to the men and women we see on television commercials, and to celebrities, asking ourselves: "How do I stack up against these guys? Am I closer to perfection than he is? Am I a slacker? Am I successful? "

This brings us back to the phenomenon of the idea of self-judgment, the uniquely human tendency to relentlessly compare ourselves to others or to some impossibly high standard and, upon concluding that we fall short, beat ourselves up. What is wrong with this strategy of self-assessment? Why shouldn't we rely upon external reinforcement for determining our self-worth?

We must realize that if we rely on the opinions of others and their standards of perfection, we are giving away our power, whether it's a compliment or criticism. And as we have already discussed, so often what people think about you is more about what they think of themselves *in relation to you* than an objective assessment of who you are in reality.

So how do we move from being an externally motivated person who judges our own self-worth based on the unreliable and subjective opinions of others to a more inner-directed self-accepting person?

The answer is to empty ourselves of attachment to concepts like perfection and constant improvement in order to move closer to acceptance and, ultimately, closer to God.

Are We Unconditionally Accepted by God?

God made us as we are. It doesn't make sense, then, that God, the creative force, would only accept us if we fulfilled conditions that made us different from the beings we are, that is, you will only be an acceptable creature if . . .

However, being accepted without conditions still means being accepted as a member of *homo sapiens:* a creature who is supposed to have wisdom, will, and choice. Part of how we are at this moment is the potential to become, to grow and mature. This potential is called forth not by a cosmic imperative, but by a cosmic invitation. God asks us to become. Become what? If we are made in the image of the Creator, that means becoming more and more loving, free, and further along the continuum from compulsion to choice.

Consider two issues here. In Matthew 5:48, Jesus tells us to "be perfect." In *what* are we to be perfect? It's important to look at the context in which Jesus says these words. If we look back ten verses or so from Matthew 5:48, we find that Jesus is at this time urging his friends to move beyond vengeance—"an eye for an eye and a tooth for a tooth"—and to go the extra mile. In verse 44 Jesus says "love your enemies," not just those who love you. So you see, in context, being perfect is most probably referring to being perfect in *love.* To grow beyond self-serving and self-aggrandizement.

The second issue is to explore how quickly one must do this. It would be wonderful if we could wave a wand and be perfect in love instantly—or at least tomorrow! But being human, that's as impossible as a little yellow tomato blossom becoming a luscious ripe tomato tomorrow, or an Olympic runner breaking the record without long training. We should be able to mature at our own pace, which need not be either instantaneous or lazy.

It is not an actual race toward either material or even moral perfection. Saint Paul picks up on this when he uses the analogy of the Olympic runner. (It is sometimes thought that Paul, being brought up in the Hellenized culture of Tarsus, would himself have been trained in the Greek games.) It's not a perishable crown of laurel, he says, that we are running for, but an imperishable, that is, a spiritual one; it is a spiritual "race" toward full humanity and mature love. So it's not how fast we run; it is not our pace that matters in the long run, so to speak, but our purpose. We are not to be in the rat race, but the human race.

In the Bible, the Greek word for perfect, *teleios*, means complete in all its parts, or full grown. You might say then that a perfect human being is a complete human being, or a mature one. The point is to be *ripe*.

We will get *old* just by breathing, but we may not necessarily get *ripe*. A green tomato left in a cupboard can eventually shrivel up and rot instead of getting succulently ripe. To stretch the image: for a tomato's ripeness, there needs to be ample moisture, soil nutrients, and sun; for human ripeness, there needs to be sufficient nurture, learning, and consciousness. A ripe human being is a conscious human being. Consciousness enables what Socrates referred to as the examined life, the only life worth living.

Major stress comes from feeling trapped between two unacceptable extremes. Constantly striving for the unattainable—perfection—is, of course, super-stress. Just sitting around and "doing nothing" is stressful and frustrating, too, because one is not living one's life: one is being lived by it. Bearing the tension between extremes can be a creative and liberating effort opening the way for other alternatives to be seen.

Of course, if you feel compelled to strive for perfection in the super-ego-driven misuse of the word, then to think of stopping the scramble and just sitting—being conscious of where and who you really are—may at first have disturbing implications, new kinds of anxiety and guilt. Questions such as "Where am I?" and "Who am I?" may arise. It is helpful to remember that questions are not demands, they are invitations. We will address how one might cope with such new feelings in chapter 8.

The point to our human existence is ultimately freedom. Freedom to respond to our life's opportunities and not feel victimized by them. Such freedom is born of a maturity of consciousness that is not ours at birth. To be fully human, we must tend the ripening of consciousness.

"Nonperformance" in a Performance World

Performance is not a condition of God's love and acceptance and should not be a criterion for our self-worth. However, human beings need work that both fulfills and challenges them. Those who have the gifts of management or leadership should learn how to use them in the way that best serves those whom they manage or lead. True leadership is not about prestige or control, but about responsibility and discernment. In this context performance does matter. *Performance* comes through Old French from the Latin, and has, among its definitions, "to furnish, complete, form thoroughly," and "carry through"—nothing about looking good or measuring up to some abstract standard. The danger in performing or winning success is when we invest our worthiness or *loveableness* in them, as in: "I will only be loved, admired, affirmed, respected, be okay, *if* . . ." It's important to remember that climbing the ladder of success does not affect a person's true worth. But, care and efficiency in our work are good and appropriately lead to promotion. Jesus said, "You have been trustworthy in a few things, I will put you in charge of many things" (Matthew 25:21). It's an issue of trust that advancement will happen naturally and not through our wheeling and dealing.

Also, challenging and creative work does not always need to be the same as a person's salaried job. An avocation, hobby, or volunteer work can provide scope for one's creative energies. But whether paid or unpaid, the unfolding of one's gifts and the maturing of one's personal power play a significant part in an individual's "ripening."

Human Ripeness and the Three Levels of Love

A mature human being is created to "ripen" in several ways: in consciousness, in the capacity to choose well, and in how to love well. Ripening in love is of paramount importance because it affects our ability to relate to ourselves, to others and to God. M. Scott Peck defined love this way in *The Road Less Traveled*: "The will to extend one's self for the purpose of nurturing one's own or another's spiritual growth."

There are many theories about human development and its stages. One particular model we have adapted to the concept of human ripeness and how it evolves we call "The Three Levels of Love." The Three Levels of Love are Narcissism, Justice, and Gift.

Level One Love—Narcissism

The human infant is like a kernel or seed that *may* ripen into a mature human person. As an infant, however, the human animal is an utter narcissist. The baby is the center of its universe—in fact, it cannot even distinguish the other from itself. The other is only a means to its end and exists only to fill its needs. The infant's cry demands, "Feed me! Pick me up! Change me! Burp me! Cuddle me!" Of course, we think this is cute in a baby—and rightly so—it's a baby's appropriate way of relating. But do you know any people who are chronologically adult to whom any other person and the universe exist only to fill their needs? Not so cute anymore. And if you give them power, watch out—you may have a Hitler or a Machiavelli. Love that is fixated on this first level of development is attachment: attachment to self-survival and self-aggrandizement. Every human being has these instincts in common with the animals.

Level Two Love—Justice

If the infant is treated as a human being and not as an object, if it receives sufficient nurture and encouragement, the seed of narcissism breaks open and begins to send out roots and shoots. Somewhere around puberty, the child will recognize himself or herself as an individual, separate from others, and can begin to perceive others as persons in their own right. If I am a person in my own right, then you are a person in your own right. At this second level of development, the concept and practice of justice is possible. If I am *I*, and you are *you*, we can negotiate. Loving at this stage means fairness and equity.

The downside of this second growth level between puberty and ripe adulthood is the tendency to need a lot of rules and laws. "This is my side of the room, and that is your side! Woe unto you if you leave your junk on my side!" "If you invite me to dinner, I will invite you back." "If you scratch my back, I'll scratch yours." Teenage gangs are characterized by rules and the breaking of rules, rewards and punishments, rigid identification with "my kind of person," and rebellion or violence against others who are different. Many chronologically adult conclaves in our society are fixated in and foster this "Us and Them" mentality. At best this stage of human development can bring about covenant; at worst, vendetta. The adverse side of negotiation and justice is vengeance: an eye for an eye, a tooth for a tooth; the *lex talionis*—the "Law of the Claw" or the law of retaliation. But the human being has the capacity for being "full grown," for true maturity. True maturity is not only freedom to choose; it is freedom from attachment to what other human beings think and the "Us or Them" mentality.

With this tendency for rules and laws in this second level comes a kind of conventional thinking that individuals and groups of individuals pass down through the ages. It is a patchwork of generalizations, old wives' tales, prejudices, group-think, gossip, tribal taboos, half-truths, and comforting lies. It is a hotbed for the nurture of "shoulds" and "oughts" and the attachment to hopeless perfectionism. It advertises itself as traditional wisdom and common sense, but it is closer to traditional tyranny and common intolerance. In fact, it is what we are calling the cultural myths. We can live in fear of its implicit or explicit censure: "If I do this, or if I don't do that, *they* will say . . ."

To react against this oppressive group-think may not yet be freedom, though it may be the first step toward freedom. A fierce reaction to anything usually implies a strong residual attachment to that thing. Freedom lies not in rebellion, but in what psychologists called "individuation." That's a fancy word meaning something like becoming your own person.

Level Three Love—Gift

If a human being evolves beyond the stage of "tit-for-tat" negotiation, she or he no longer needs to be ruled by tribal loyalties, peer pressure, or the conventional "should" system. Discernment then has developed to the point where the person can see what *is* instead of what is generally *supposed to be* and act out of choice rather than ignorance or compulsion. There is no longer the need for certainty—that if I scratch your back you will scratch mine; that if I am good I will be rewarded. If certainty and reciprocity, and even fairness, are no longer demanded, one can live by possibilities in a dynamic structure of change. It means that risk is possible. A person can choose a course of action in any circumstance, not because of any external stress or pressure, but because he or she chooses to live that way. Of course, this way of living implies taking a certain responsibility for one's life, and that means there is no one "out there" to blame. But it also means freedom. The freedom to be one's own self and to let others be themselves. To love on this third level has ceased to be attachment and has become mature intimacy.

No one is ever perfectly ripe. *Nobody lives on Level Three all the time.* We are all constantly making a mess of things, doing things we regret, "blowing it." To say nothing of regression. But every moment of the process can be used to learn, and the truth will lead us to freedom and wisdom.

The Movement toward "Ripeness"

Becoming a full human being is a cooperative project. An atheist might call it a combination of the luck of the draw—gene pool, early environment, educational advantages—and the individual's commitment to seek the truth about things. A Christian might call it the interaction of God's grace and a person's free will. A partnership. Or better, a friendship: "I do not call you servants any longer . . . but I have called you friends" (John 15:15). The age-old dilemma in this endeavor is how much should the individual be responsible for and how much should the Holy Spirit be responsible for? Pelagius, a much-maligned Irish monk of the fifth century who got an entire heresy named for him, taught that "getting somewhere" spiritually is all up to us. Of course, there was the *opposite* extreme. Jansenism, the heresy named after Cornelis Jansen (1585–1638), taught among other things that freedom of the will was nonexistent. More or less the "Why do anything?" approach to spirituality. The way of love, human or divine, is neither doing it all yourself, nor having it all done for you.

What can a person do to cooperate in this ripening process? Basically there are three things: try to stay awake, try to see things clearly, and try to grapple with the question of how to accept the unacceptable.

Spiritual awakening usually comes at certain moments of insight and is like a breakthrough to another level of consciousness. It is an "Oh, I get it!" moment. Staying awake is the practice of staying conscious. It is the hard job of not falling back into sloppy thinking, stereotyping, generalizing, and denial.

Trying to see things clearly means seeing things as they are—not as we are taught they ought to be or should be. There are three kinds of people who best see things and people the way they "really are": children before they go to school, great artists, and contemplatives. Children in their rich fantasies, great artists in shape and color, and contemplatives in their openness to mystery see beyond surface appearance to essence and potential. As we grow and ripen into our true selves, we can practice looking at things—a sky or a human form—as it really is.

The third way to cooperate with ripening is to grapple with accepting what seems unacceptable. This is very hard. One important distinction is that to accept a certain reality is not necessarily to like or condone it. Really accepting what *is* establishes the best first step to understanding what it might become and to discern your own part in that becoming. Or accepting that you don't have any part in this particular unacceptable matter and just letting it go—emptying oneself of the need to fix or change or convert.

The disciplines of meditation and prayer are splendid means to help us stay conscious, see with more clarity, and grapple with accepting and dealing with the more difficult realities of our lives. Psychotherapy is also a fine tool to help us wake up out of false dreamy states of mind and come to clarity so that we can mature in holy wisdom and right choice of action.

When we realize that Divine perfection has to do with love, compassion, mercy, and justice, not with what grade we get or how much money we make, or how famous we are, then we are maturing—we are becoming ripe as we empty our attachment to a concept like perfection. Our vessel can be closer to being filled with God.

CHAPTER TWO

The Myth of Control

Myth: It is not only possible to completely control one's own destiny but also it is our responsibility to do so.

Truth: The process of living in the world is about interacting in harmony with others and with the rest of creation. Working hard to discern when to hold on and when to let go is the only thing over which we have control.

If one of the pervasive beliefs we internalize is the idea of moving toward perfection, a concept right next to that idea is the myth of control: the idea that if we pay enough attention to details and have clear goals, a strong will, and a relentless drive, we can become master of our own fate. After all, civilizations throughout history were established on human beings' ability to conquer, organize, and control their natural environments. Our history is filled with stories of the hero overcoming impossible odds to climb a mountain, or cross an ocean, or discover a cure for a deadly disease, or overcome an oppressive regime to bring freedom to the land.

In this chapter, we are going to look at how the belief of control gets installed into our consciousness, how it can lead to enormous stress, and how we can begin to look at the issue of control as a kind of give and take or dance between ourselves as individual vessels and the creative force we call God.

Family Systems and the Myth of Control

It should not come as a great shock that the myth of control has been installed into our belief system since childhood. After all, if we really are, as Sartre noted, creatures who want to become God, then a logical strategy would be to begin the long road toward the infinite by gaining control of one's immediate environment.

Parents and children embark on an epic battle of control, especially during the teenage years, as the child attempts to gain a separate identity from his or her parents, while the parents try, often in the best interest of the child, to teach the rules of society so the child will conform enough to survive. These struggles mirror the overall struggle humans face in wanting freedom on the one hand and approval on the other. The consequence often is the attempt to control each other to preserve individual freedom. It appears to become a sort of zero-sum game in which freedom for *me* depends on the denial of freedom for *you*.

This "zero-sum" society is a place where we learn we have only two choices: winning and losing. Or, to control or be controlled.

As we grow up, we are often taught within the family that there is only so much success in the world, and we have to hustle to get a piece of it. This is consistent with the zero-sum idea. We begin to look at others not in terms of how we can engage in a meaningful and mutually supportive relationship, but rather as threats to our success. If there is only so much success to go around, then it would be stupid of us to think of sharing with others or offering to help others, unless of course there was a clear quid pro quo: I do this for you, you do that for me. To view others as objects to control is not exactly something that nurtures human relationship, nor is it what God wants for us in this life.

But it is a reality that modern life has created barriers to individual growth as well as to the growth of human relationships. For if each individual feels compelled to get the upper hand and have power over the other, mature relationships are almost impossible to achieve. Our attachment to control gets in the way of pursuing our God-given right to freedom and love. The antidote to this myth of control may lie in discerning when to hold on and when to let go.

Peer Groups and the Myth of Control

The first encounter with control one has outside the family is in school, where elaborate systems with bells and lines and report cards and rules about talking and raising one's hand predominate. The goal of such schoolyard rules is on one level to more efficiently deliver educational services to children. On a more reflective level, it is to teach us the importance of control.

The games we play as kids further demonstrate the payoff that is available to those who gain the upper hand and have power others. On the playground, a game like "keep-away" teaches the concept of control. Two kids play catch with some object, usually a ball of some kind, and a third child tries to intercept it. The object of the game for the two with the ball is to keep it. The object of the game for the third person is to intercept the ball and "gain control." A board game like *Monopoly* is all about systematically buying up all the property on the board so that when other players land on the piece of real estate you own, you can charge them rent. Ultimately, by owning all the real estate, you gain a monopoly and win the game by obtaining total control. *Risk* is another game that has control as a central theme, only there the stakes are even higher: win the game and take control of the entire world!

We become filled with the notion that we are to take responsibility for our lives, and it is a central tenet of the American Dream that, like Horatio Alger, we can become successful by the sweat of our brow. But the path to success is not very clear, nor is it necessarily easy—and it takes control. Hence you see fast-track baby boomers sitting in restaurants or in their cars during a traffic jam or in line at the grocery store talking on their cell phones or consulting their PDAs. If we ever hope to gain control in this chaotic world, the logic goes, we must at least stay connected to the people and organizations that will take us to this fictitious place of control over our world.

This kind of approach is not lost on kids who are watching and imitating their parents (and television commercials) at every turn. Hence it is not unusual to see fifteen-year-old kids with all kinds of gadgets trying to keep up with parents who are running as fast as they can, trying to keep a handle on their lives.

Where the myth of control can have dire consequences for people is when they lose any sense of balance and become obsessed. Addiction is the ultimate manifestation of such obsession. Unable to strike a balance between holding on and letting go, the addict tends to anesthetize himself or herself seemingly as the only escape from striving to control the uncontrollable.

We are even told that our relationship with God is something over which we can and should have control. If I am not experiencing the kind of rich prayer life that I am encouraged to believe is possible, then I must try that much harder by spending two or three hours a day in meditation or prayer or until I break through.

Knowing when to hold on and when to let go is the challenge. We may believe that everything we do and everything that happens to us is our responsibility and our fault—like we are the playwright and everyone around us is an actor in our play.

However, this is a narcissistic, self-involved kind of worldview—unfortunately, we're not alone in this since there are plenty of people around us buying into the same myth.

Culture and the Myth of Control

Just as marketers seek to attract our consumer dollars by claiming their product will move us closer to perfection, they claim we can regain control of our lives through the products we buy. Whether it is regaining control of a weight problem, regaining control of a cigarette habit, eliminating drug and alcohol abuse, regaining control of relationships with a spouse or a teenager—for every aspect of our out-of-control life, the marketplace has a product that will put us back in control.

Convinced that we have to be thin, rich, powerful, happily married, and successful and that all of it is in our control, we place enormous pressure on ourselves every single day to perform in such a way as to make all of it happen. And we look to the marketplace to provide us with the tools we need to get there: a faster computer, handheld gadgets for every form of communication, a fancy car with all the latest technological advances, books promising the "seven ways to control your financial future" or the "ten immutable laws to help you win."

But how are we to know when and with how much vigor we should engage in life and when we should let go and let the forces over which we have no control prevail? How do I empty myself of the myth that I have to control everything in my environment and yet know when it is appropriate to act?

Control Isn't All Bad

It's important to remember that when we try to control everything, we are playing God. The thing is, it doesn't work to try to control *everything*, though it does work for us to control *some* things. For example, a young woman was in a convent to try her vocation and was struggling with new geography, new climate, new relationships, new customs, and new authority structures. One morning she was asked how she was doing. "I feel a lot better this morning," she said. "This morning I organized my underwear drawer." That was the one thing in her environment she felt she had some kind of control over, which actually helped her deal with the larger issues.

The desire for control shows itself at peculiar times. A poignant example is one from a terminally ill sister in the convent. One of her household jobs had been to bundle and tie up the old newspapers and magazines for recycling. One day, she had asked two visitors to do this job. As the visitors were tying the string around a bundle of magazines, the sister cried out, "Tighter, tighter!" They pulled the string tighter, but apparently not tight enough before she was out of bed and limping toward the table where they were working, still saying, "Tighter, tighter!" The desire for control exerts itself mightily—if we can't be in control of our life span, we can at least be in control of *something*.

Art and literature are examples of our desire for control that work. We cannot get our heads around the seemingly terrible randomness of life, so we put a frame around it, or, as Aristotle said of drama, we give it a beginning, a middle, and an end. Whether it is a happy ending or a tragic ending, the effect is that wild chaos is corralled and things are under control again. King Oedipus suffers for his tragic mistakes, and order is restored to the land.

Control isn't all bad, but excessive attempts at control—"trying to control everything in my world"—don't work. Desire for inordinate control stems from fear or insecurity. It is a vain attempt at sticking your finger in the dike against the raging flood of reality.

The Concept of Surrender

The concept of surrender needs some thinking about, some "unpacking." True surrender or emptying isn't giving up. It is an act of doing, not of being done to. If I am *forced* to give up or surrender something—my property, my rights, my life—that puts me in the victim position, and my response is submission or conciliation.

Being a victim obviously is very bad news. It is not only bad for the victim but also for the oppressor. The victim stance is an adversarial one; the victim feels "It's them against me" just as much as any warring party. Victimization breeds rage that may prove to be impotent, but which creates a hostile atmosphere. It may result in hatred, which has been described as "drinking poison and hoping the other person will get sick."

The key to true, life-giving emptiness or surrender is *choice*. The minute you feel other people or external sources are forcing you to surrender, you become a victim. Surrender is a kind of giving, and all true gifts must be freely made.

Surrender must be freely chosen, and it must be realistic. It is critical to remember that *you cannot give what you do not have*. You can't pour milk out of a pitcher that doesn't have any milk in it. The people of the First Covenant knew that if you wanted to surrender something, to make a sacrifice to God, it must be the *best* you had: full, perfect, unblemished. In true sacrifice, oblation must come before immolation (thank offering before the sacrificial death).

People have trouble with the concept of surrender. Many women say they have for so long been made to surrender, by which they mean to comply, to capitulate, to give in, that they will not, in conscience, do it any longer. They want to feel what it's like to hold on, to be in control of their lives. Many men say that surrender is really hard for *them* because they've been brought up in a culture in which men especially are pressured into always holding on, winning, being top dog, and being in control. In that mind-set, no kind of surrender is seen as an option. These women and men need to experience more fullness before they are ready to empty. Both groups may need, for example, to come to a desire for the fullness of justice and a sense of self-worth, for a fullness of emotional range and a ripened compassion. Again, you can't give away what you don't have. You can't make a real choice until you have real alternatives.

So, why does surrender work? One of the most cogent answers of our time is to be found in the wisdom of the twelve-step programs. "We admitted we were powerless . . . made a decision to turn our will and our lives over . . ." The only real point of surrender, of letting go of control, is to move closer to truth; the truth is we are never in control of the cosmos. To pretend to be is to move away from truth toward lie.

Caught in the Trap of Needing to Control

The control trap starts very early in life. Learning to control some things, like our sphincters and certain expressions of our rage in the terrible twos, is very useful in the process of becoming civilized and mature. But there is an aspect that is counterproductive and dangerous. When an individual feels "caught in a trap," the emotions usually aroused are not only anxiety but also desperation and rage. (If one is trapped or caged up too long, of course, the emotions can change into misery and despair.) If people get trapped in the conviction that they should or must control their environment, they may come to the point that if they are *not* in control, they don't know what they are worth; some simply may not know that they *are*, that they exist.

When an animal—even the human animal—is trapped, it may become dangerous to itself, and to others. Stress and fear easily lead into rage and hostility. The cornered rat bares its teeth and gets ready to fight to the death. Watch out when a person driven to control feels threatened or trapped.

Called to Lead—Not Control

We need control in some areas, and some people do have a calling and a gift for controlling or ordering situations in a most effective way. Some people are called to leadership. Leadership by definition implies working well in community. We don't walk in the world totally alone—captain of our fate and master of our soul—although often it feels like that. We should call the proper use of such a gift of leadership *authority* rather than *control*. The word authority can be traced back to Latin *augere*, meaning "to increase, produce." Authority, rightly exercised, increases responsibility in others; self-serving control diminishes it. A great CEO encourages and increases creative effort and responsibility in those around her or him. True authority comes out of personal fullness and the will to make order out of chaos. Driven control comes out of insecurity and hidden self-doubt and the need to adjust the environment for one's own self-aggrandizement. Control by force or manipulation might be called the junk food of power; it may satisfy the moment's ambition, but it won't effect any lasting good.

A shepherd may be said to control a flock. If the shepherd is a true shepherd and not a hired hand, the flock will be led out of care for its welfare and not out of the control needs of the shepherd. It is good to remember that the ability to order things well is a gift—but not necessarily a better gift than others.

Like any addiction, control *seems* to fill a need. The bottle, the cigarette, the needle, or the ability to put down or fire a subordinate makes one feel temporarily less lonely, less ineffective, or less vulnerable. The idea of letting go involves risk and fear. People ask, "What if I let go and don't make it to the top of my profession, lose people's admiration, lose my own sense of myself, completely fall apart? Is there any guarantee that

I will not fall into the pit of despair—of no-self?" One faces a crisis of trust. A wise person was once asked, "How many battles can you lose and still win the war?" The answer? "All of them."

Sometimes when a person begins the hard transition from attempted control over his or her environment toward the freedom of surrender, there is fear, or at least an uncomfortable insecurity. In the end, risking without being *certain* and breaking the addiction to control most often ushers in good news.

It is not hard to see why a human being becomes or stays addicted. It is *hard* to quit, to surrender. What must be given up is the lie that this substance or this behavior will do away with, or at least dull, the existential pain. Ultimately lies don't work. The truth will make you free, but first it will make you miserable! The crucial point is trust that it will indeed and finally make us free.

Mutuality

Neither over-control nor unwilling surrender is respectful of the other. The story of a woman and ballroom dancing illustrates this well. As a child, the woman was sent to dancing school to learn ballroom dancing. They were a class of awkward twelve-and thirteen-year-olds trying to learn the steps and treading on each others' toes. The better she learned the steps, the more she tried to push and pull her partner around. Naturally he was trying to do the same thing. Being the boy, he was supposed to lead in the ways of ballroom dancing, but the young girl felt he was doing it all wrong. Consequently, they kept trying to go in different directions, holding on to each other tightly in order to push or nudge the other. It was a vain attempt to control.

With time and long practice, the girl grew to become quite a good ballroom dancer and one evening went dancing with a friend. She noticed that as she followed his lead, he hardly had to lead at all; she could barely feel his hand on her shoulder or his fingers touching hers. After a while it was as if she knew instinctively which way they would move or turn—they were so at one with each other and with the music.

Finally it seemed as if it were no longer clear who was leading; sometimes he would initiate the direction, and other times she would make the slightest of movements that would become a change of direction or a turn. Yet, he was still formally "leading." It was as if by some sort of mystical delegation she could indicate, "What if we went this way?" and they would.

That experience is a good analogy for the way our human spirit "dances" with the Holy Spirit (or if you like, with the Cosmic Energy or the Great Unknown). We never formally take the lead, but when we have lived enough and practiced to the point where practice is transcended, then it can seem that our own will is truly one with divine reality. This may be what is special about the prayers of people who are full enough to choose to be empty. Perhaps their "What if we went this way?" touches God, and God responds out of abundance: "Why not; let's do." This is the very opposite of trying to control God's will by telling God what to do. There is a wonderful saying in an old book, *Triumphant in Suffering: A Study in Reparation,* by W. F. Adams, S.S.J.E. and Gilbert Shaw: "The power of prayer can never be exaggerated. It does not change the will of God, but it releases it."

Making Room for Grace

A way to think about grace is that it is the way divine love is manifested and becomes effective in our lives. Classically there are two kinds of grace. The first is called prevenient and suggests the idea and wish to do what is good; the second is cooperating and gives the power to do it. If we see grace in this way, as the active power of Love's divine energy in our lives, then it's not too hard to see why our attempts to control things on our own might thwart or not leave room for that power. The attachment to personal control, the use of power for self-aggrandizement—these leave no room for grace, for the spirit. And it takes two to tango.

CHAPTER THREE

The Myth of Accumulation

Myth: The person with the most stuff wins.

Truth: The accumulation of wealth is only a tiny fraction of what it means to lead a fulfilling life. There are many different levels of desire and happiness, of which accumulation is only one.

The first order of business is to define what we mean by the word "accumulation." In general, it means to gather, collect, or pile up. It derives from the Latin *cumulare*, to heap. What we mean by it is that there is a strong current in our culture that suggests that anything worth striving for in the material world is worth accumulating in large quantities. In America, and increasingly in other industrialized countries, *more is better*.

This concept of more is better is not limited just to material wealth or material possessions but can also mean the accumulation of all kinds of things: honors, public adulation, children, romantic conquests, or, as Thorstein Veblen put it in *The Theory of the Leisure Class*, anything that facilitates "conspicuous consumption." We are a society that likes to hoard and collect material possessions in quantities that would boggle the minds of our forebears. And we do so because ever since we were little, we were taught that fulfillment comes from such accumulation. This chapter will look at how we come to believe such things and how counterproductive such beliefs are in terms of helping us achieve a fulfilling life.

Family Systems and the Myth of Accumulation

Lest there be any doubt about how Americans have come to view the importance of wealth accumulation in the last twenty-five years or so, consider this statistic from just a decade ago: a study asked, "If you could change one thing about your life, what would it be?" Sixty-four percent or almost two out of three said, "More wealth." Numerous other studies have asked Americans what "quality of life" means to them, and the most frequent response has referred to some kind of income security. A poll of baby boomer-aged schoolteachers asked whether or not their students were significantly different than they had been as kids. Seventy-six percent of the teachers felt their students were more materialistic than they were as kids.

These kinds of polls should come as no surprise to anyone who has been paying attention to the messages we have been digesting from our families, friends, and from society. According to Martha Rogers and Don Peppers, authors of *The One to One Future*, American businesses produce between 2,000 to 3,000 commercial messages *every day* for every man, woman, and child in the United States. We are literally bombarded with the notion that having and spending money will greatly improve our lives.

Post-World War II families have occupied themselves with accumulation. Parents reward children for doing well in school or doing chores around the house by giving some material possession. It doesn't take long for any of us to figure out that in a market economy, stuff matters—a lot.

Money is equated with ultimate power and success. Wealth accumulation is the way we show love for each other through the acquisition and transfer of material possessions. Thus at Christmastime, we exchange a ridiculous number of gifts in a genuine effort to show love for each other. This may partially explain the unprecedented credit card debt Americans are accumulating. Since this system of showing love is pervasive in the United States, one can only imagine how heart-wrenching it is for the growing number of people in poverty to live through a holiday season with a limited ability to show their children and each other love in this way.

Since the predominant thing a majority of Americans would change about their life is more wealth, this suggests they have been socialized to spend most of their time striving to accumulate money. And, they pursue wealth because it carries with it the promise of happiness. Unfortunately, a significant body of research suggests wealth accumulation alone does not lead to more happiness. According to data from the National Opinion Research Center, during the years between 1957 and 1990 when per capita wealth was doubling, the number of people reporting they were "very happy" actually declined slightly from 34 percent to 29 percent. Thus, we may have doubled our per capita wealth, but the number of those "very happy" went down.

Further, researchers suggest that Americans born after 1946 are *ten times* more likely to experience depression in their lives than those born prior to 1946. And when juxtaposed with the data about wealth increases, this finding raises serious questions about the value of wealth in contributing to mental health.

Despite the material things surrounding them, many kids are not happy. Why? Part of the reason is that what they really need the most is a loving adult to guide them through the crucial teen years. But even in nuclear families (those that haven't exploded), both mom and dad are working all the time in order to afford the stuff we have become convinced we need. As the pace of society quickens and shrinking time forces families to make hard choices about how to spend their time, the quest for material possessions has left family relationships in the dust for many Americans.

Peer Groups and the Myth of Accumulation

The primary way that accumulation manifests itself in the context of peer influences is in the comparison game. Kids at the teenage level are so concerned with the way their peers view them that they become obsessed with wearing the right clothes and having the right techno gadgets. We may argue that rather than being too materialistic, we may actually not be materialistic enough in the sense of really valuing things. There is so much of everything in and around us that any one item becomes devalued.

But, something more insidious about the myth of accumulation exists as it relates to peer influence. Since material possessions seem to be the pre-eminent path to esteem and acceptance, money becomes the magic elixir without which one will suffer. Individual relationships in this kind of environment become characterized by conditional love. Genuine, accepting, unconditional relationships become a measure of one's naiveté.

But it doesn't need to be this way. We don't need to make the accumulation of wealth the only measure of worth.

Culture and the Myth of Accumulation

It is an old and almost worn-out idea that the media and specifically advertisers are the culprits for our over-consumption and over-accumulation. And while it is true that Americans in effect brainwash themselves by choosing to watch four or five hours of commercial-laden television per day, our desire to accumulate may have deeper roots. Television advertising and the retail-driven consumer society are really just symptoms of a deep yearning we all have for love and acceptance. And because we are either unable or unwilling to think more reflectively about why we do things like run up large balances on our credit cards and purchase huge quantities of unnecessary stuff, accumulation becomes the only apparent avenue to getting what we want on a deep level. Hence we get the phrase "retail therapy" as a way of describing the root of many consumers' motivation in the malls.

Some people will say they go shopping just because it is an activity they enjoy. Others are more direct about its palliative effects. "I had a bad day yesterday and so I am going to go do some damage to my credit card." "No one else is going to be nice to me today, so I am going to go do something nice for myself and buy a new dress."

The problem with accumulation as a means of satisfying deeper types of yearnings is that it simply doesn't work, or if it does work, it doesn't work for long. Joe Dominquez and Vicki Robin in their book *Your Money or Your Life*, describe a concept called "The Fulfillment Curve." The idea is that when one starts out in life, one assumes that each additional material possession will result in a corresponding rise in one's fulfillment or happiness. And for quite a while, this is what happens. But as Dominquez and Robin point out, as we continue to acquire material possessions, the curve begins to flatten and pretty soon we are buying more and more stuff and it is not producing more fulfillment. At some critical level, each additional purchase not only fails to increase fulfillment but also actually lowers it. This is because we are spending so much time working to pay for and maintain things that it is reducing our happiness.

Numerous studies suggest that accumulation of wealth alone will not result in limitless increases in fulfillment and happiness. If we were to graph the research cited earlier about the doubling of per capita wealth versus polls which gauge individual happiness, it would look almost exactly the same as the Dominquez/Robin Fulfillment Curve. Wealth increases but those reporting they are very happy flattens and starts to decline slightly. Factor in the huge increases in those people reporting bouts with depression, and you have a strong indication that declines in happiness may continue despite increases in wealth.

So how do we make sense of all of this? Why is it that we start out so thoroughly convinced that we are going to become happy by accumulating wealth, only to find that there is a limit to the extent to which it will get us there? It's useful to look at the four levels of human happiness, which we have adapted from the work of Robert Spitzer.

The four levels of human desire can be condensed rather simply:

Level Four—Ultimate Reality

Level Three —Good Beyond Self

Level Two—Ego Satisfaction

Level One —Physical Pleasure

The way to view these levels of happiness is in terms of how deep, wide, and long the happiness payoff is for each. In general, Level One and Two activities offer more immediate gratification, which wears off more quickly. Levels Three and Four tend to have a slower payoff, but the rewards are deeper and more long lasting.

Level One is the pleasure produced by an external stimulus like the sensory stimulation of drinking a latte or the satisfaction derived from owning a luxury car. This level is where we would put most of the accumulated possessions that we have been discussing. Certainly buying and owning things like new trendy clothes and jewelry or a bigger house in a more upscale neighborhood would be done pursuant to this desire.

Level Two of happiness is about ego gratification, such as achievements or recognition, or power and control. We would accumulate degrees, awards, and impressive job titles to address this type of desire. Accumulating expensive things might also serve to satisfy this level. It is also the stimulus behind the wearing of "social masks" and trying to lose weight and looking young in order to compare favorably to others and gain their approval.

Level Three of happiness is the pleasure derived from serving others beyond oneself; it is making a contribution to society. Level Three activities are likely to generate more lasting fulfillment and happiness than levels one or two, but each level represents legitimate human needs. By extending oneself beyond one's immediate needs, wants, and ego, one is beginning to participate in the broader context of life. It is also Level Three that cultivates our relationships with others and helps build social networks of community. Research indicates that people who interact with others regularly are more fulfilled or happy than those who do not. Extroverts always score higher on happiness survey instruments than introverts.

Level Four of happiness is the pleasure to be derived from being associated with the infinite, something which is transcendent and of ultimate significance. It is moving into the realm of higher consciousness, where the broader context is glimpsed, however fleetingly. Level Four is about recognizing that there is a bigger universe that we often cannot fully grasp but to which we are nevertheless connected.

THE FOUR LEVELS OF HUMAN HAPPINESS

Level Four — *Ultimate or Infinite Reality*
The focus is on understanding the broader
context against which one exists.

Level Three — *Good beyond Self*
The focus is on connection to something other
than one's own needs and expectations.

Level Two — *Ego Satisfaction*
The focus is on competition, winning, and
on reenforcement from others.

Level One — *Physical Pleasure*
The focus is on physical pleasure
and satisfaction.

These four levels of happiness are useful as a way of putting into context one of the reasons accumulation as a way of making us happy is, in fact, a myth. While material wealth is indeed a legitimate source of pleasure and happiness, it is only one level of happiness and the bottom level at that.

The trick to operating within these four realms is to stand on the ground of one level, with a vigilant eye on the horizon of the next level. Understanding the limited nature of materialism and its accumulation is the key to not getting stuck in it. Likewise, realizing that one's ego needs are important but not the sole point of human existence is crucial to increasing the extent to which life can be fulfilling. Too often we get stuck by asking materialism (Level One) to do something for us it was not designed to do (provide ultimate happiness and meaning).

In order to avoid becoming stuck in any of the levels of one's desire, we must understand the context, the infinite horizon against which we live and breathe. As Frederick Buechner said in *Wishful Thinking: A Seeker's ABC*, idolatry is "ascribing absolute value to something of relative worth." Part of what ails us may be that we are filled with beliefs that do precisely that: place ultimate value on things of relative value. The mistake is to believe "things" have absolute value. Too many of us are stuck going back and forth between Levels One and Two, not understanding the importance of Levels Three and Four, because our culture places so little emphasis on them.

The Clamor for More Stuff

"More stuff" is very attractive. You might say it is irresistible. Evidence of the attraction goes back to Adam and Eve. They had a whole garden of fruit trees to eat from. Why did they want *one more?* When Eve "saw that the tree was good for food, and that it was a delight to the eyes and that the tree was to be desired to make one wise, she took of its fruit and ate." *More stuff* always shows itself as good and delightful and something we need to make us better, greater, happier, richer, or wiser. The desired object sets up in us a mental static that drowns out any rational knowledge. We can't or won't hear that in the *long run* inordinate amassing of things will make us not more fulfilled, but diminished.

King Midas, for instance, wanted more gold. Gold is by nature good and delightful; it's both very attractive and very useful. The gods granted Midas's wish that everything he touched would turn to gold. His delight lasted only one day. That evening when he sat down to dinner he realized with a shock that his food and drink also turned to gold. He had to go back to the gods begging them to take their gift away.

Human beings have a built-in desire for what is good. One problem comes in discerning between short-term good and long-term good (or intrinsic and extrinsic values). For instance, a young person is faced with the choice of studying or going to the movies. Going to the movies has intrinsic value; it is seen as good in itself. The young person may, however, choose to stay home and study because of the extrinsic values of a better job and a fuller life in the future.

It's hard for us to discern between immediate and lasting good, particularly in the heat of the moment. Maybe it's even harder to choose between that which seems good in our immaturity and the good we are called to choose out of our "ripeness." What we clamor for out of infant narcissism is very different from that of ripened wisdom when we have learned how to delay gratification. One reason we continually clamor for more stuff when it clearly is not making us happier is that we either get stuck in, or regress back to, Levels One or Two of the Human Happiness

Scale. If people come to the realization that, in the long run, Levels One and Two are not going to be enough to make them happy, there would not be so many instances of tragic despair.

The Scarcity Syndrome

Perhaps the fear, and in many cases the experience, of deprivation, of having everything one prizes taken away underlies the scarcity syndrome, which leads to accumulating. Children who live in fear that anything they really want or want to do will be denied them grow up feeling deprived. As adults they find it very difficult to throw anything away (the "pack rat") and they strive constantly for honors, recognition, and accolades. It seems that because they did not have enough in the past, nothing is enough now. The pack rat is motivated by past deprivation.

Another manifestation of the scarcity syndrome is the collector. Consider the example of a woman living in New York City during the 40s and 50s who was unable to enjoy a professional career because of the cultural norms of the times. Since she was deprived of professional opportunities, she spent an inordinate amount of time collecting and accumulating pre-Columbian gold. While the collection she so thoroughly strove to acquire was left at her death to a museum where others now may enjoy its beauty, the collecting—the accumulation—did not seem to make her a happier or more fulfilled person.

Then there is the person who hoards; hoarding carries a sense of secrecy and greed. Hoarders squirrel their stuff away, they stockpile it so that no one will deprive them of it. Deprivation breeds a scarcity mentality, and fear of scarcity, in turn, breeds an inordinate need to accumulate and then to defend the hoard. No matter how much precious stuff the

hoarder can pile up, the fear of scarcity persists, and it persists in depriv-
ing the person of contentment, and even more, of happiness.

The classic example of the false promise of accumulating comes from
the Bible:

> The land of a rich man produced abundantly. And he thought to him-
> self, "What should I do, for I have no place to store my crops?" Then he
> said, "I will do this: I will pull down my barns and build larger ones, and
> there I will store all my grain and my goods. And I will say to my soul,
> Soul, you have ample goods laid up for many years; relax, eat, drink, be
> merry." But God said to him, "You fool! This very night your life is being
> demanded of you. And the things you have prepared, whose will they
> be?" (Luke 12:16-20)

No matter how much precious stuff we pile up, it's a myth that we
receive contentment, safety, and, even more, happiness. Shakespeare
wrote: "Golden lads and girls all must, / As chimney sweepers, come
to dust."

A true danger is in investing one's worth or identity in something
external to oneself: the golden throne, the gold medal, the gold Cadillac
can become more than status symbols; such acquisitions, or what they
signify, may take over a part of who the owners *are* to the world,
and most dangerously, who they are to themselves. They equate their
worth with what they possess. What would they do if they lost these
things? Who would they be? Who would remember them after they
are gone?

Often, when people become aware and ask themselves these questions,
it does happen that they begin to grieve the loss of these ego props. Such
grief is realistic. However, the "good news" eventually surfaces. The first
part of the good news is that the *awareness* of the problem is the most
effective step toward its resolution. Second, awareness will lead to freedom—in this case, freedom from misplaced attachment to *things*.

Assuming moderation and sharing, good things are created to be delighted in, and our appropriate response when we become free of misplaced attachment is enjoyment in them but the freedom to be without them. We can then be grateful but also free to be generous.

Achieving Balance

It is *possible* for a person to continue to accumulate and still grow spiritually. But it isn't easy. Scholars through the ages have fretted over Matthew 19:24; Mark 10:25; and Luke 18:25. Some suggest, for example, that "the eye of a needle" spoken of was the name of a very narrow gate in the city wall through which it was impossible for a heavily laden camel to pass—something like one of our overpasses that can only accommodate vehicles under a certain height. In any case, taken in context, the point of the story is to show that having many possessions or continuing to accumulate, may pose a strong, if not an irresistible, distraction to finding the true treasure of one's life.

We all must discern for ourselves where the heart is: which of the world's goods are nurturing to spiritual growth and which diminish spirit, even while fattening bodies or egos or wallets. There is a fine description of the distractions of possessions in the Deuterocanonical book of Ecclesiasticus. It also includes the statement there that it is *possible* to be rich and also to be blessed:

> Wakefulness over wealth wastes away one's flesh, and anxiety about it drives away sleep . . . One who loves gold will not be justified; one who pursues money will be led astray by it . . . [But] Blessed is the rich person who is found blameless, and who does not go after gold. Who is he, that we may praise him? For he has done wonders among his people. (Ecclesiasticus 31:1-9)

Accumulation involves attachment, and attachment is a major hindrance to the spirit. If anything—any *thing* or *things*—fills our thoughts and steals our attention from our deepest desires, then we become slaves to the myth of accumulation.

It is perhaps not so much a question of balance but of attitude. That is, it may be less important whether we have much or little, plain things or costly, than whether we can sit lightly to them or, on the contrary, hoard them for purposes of self-worth, the approval of others, or greed born of the scarcity myth.

As our culture and the human race as a whole ripens, it is to be hoped that we will collectively as well as individually receive and cherish the gift to live a more simple life. If we fail to simplify our consumer demands and distribute the world's wealth more equitably, we will continue to deprive huge segments of the world's populations of even basic needs. If the human race doesn't move up the happiness scale to considerations of "Good Beyond Self," our heedless accumulation and consumption of the world's resources promises dire consequences.

In *The Gift*, Lewis Hyde gives the contrast of our prevailing consumer society with the gift society of the early Native American people. When, for instance, they needed to consume the bison, they first gave the beast their worshipful respect and gratitude, and the bison in mutual gift offered its life to them for food.

But we are part of *our* society, and there is a limit to how simple we may be and still remain a part of it. It is crucial to remember that guilt and beating up on ourselves will not in itself help anything. What will help is awareness, acceptance of the realities involved, and doing what we can.

Perhaps living simply is rather naive in that it seems to negate the complexity of living in our present-day world. True simplicity sometimes takes a lifetime of conscious concern and action to achieve; simplicity, which is informed by experience and chosen in grace, will lead to fulfillment.

To the degree that it is joyfully chosen, simplicity can be a way of emptying the vessel in order for there to be space for joy and peace. Happiness is a by-product neither of acquisition nor of deprivation; happiness is a by-product of the mutual self-gift of mature love. Balance is the key.

Accumulation of Praise

A primary reason for accumulating things like praise from others is that it provides us with love that we crave. And while God unconditionally loves us, God is very often a silent God. So to give up the need for approval from others in order to listen for approval from a silent God is scary and often unfulfilling. We must watch for the preoccupation with praise from others that can drown out the voice of God.

It is true that our God is most often a God of silence and invisibility. In 1 Kings 19:12 we read: "But the LORD was not in the fire; and after the fire a sound of sheer silence." And in Isaiah 45:15, "Truly, you are a God who hides himself, O God of Israel, the Savior." It is a built-in part of our humanity to yearn to see the face of Divine Compassion and to hear the voice of Love. Because we might not see and hear God, we quite simply turn to others for that need to be filled.

There is a story that is connected with writer Madeleine L'Engle. It's the story of a small boy who was afraid of the dark. One night he kept thinking of excuses to keep his mother with him. "I want a glass of milk," and then when the milk was gone, "I have to go potty," and after that was done, "Read me another story." Finally the patient mother said, "That's enough, now try to go to sleep." "But, it's dark," came the quavering little voice, "don't leave me alone." "You don't have to be afraid," said the mother gently, "you're not alone, God is with you." After a moment the child answered, "But I want someone *with skin on!*"

It is human to want "someone with skin on." (Perhaps that is the reason for the Incarnation.) And it is not a bad thing to desire people's love and their good opinions of us, any more than it is a bad thing to desire the material goods we have talked about. The trouble comes when we accumulate human praise and good opinions *as a substitute* for God's love, for true friendship, or for our own self-acceptance. We are then, once again, stockpiling treasures that may fill us but not nourish us in the long run. And the anxiety that attends our driven, or even addictive, need for these good opinions will keep us from freedom.

The Road Less Material

There is no virtue in emptying for the sake of emptying. First, let's look at what we're emptying ourselves *of*. There are basic things we need to empty ourselves of to find our true purpose. By ridding ourselves of these, the myth of accumulation can be overcome.

1. The biases, prejudices, cultural lies and images that keep us from seeing the truth about ourselves and others.

2. Our own predetermined and unyielding agenda.

3. The need to control, fix, organize, or convert oneself, another or a group.

4. The fear that keeps us from surrender to a higher power (of which the twelve-step groups speak).

5. The demand for certainty, security, and perfection.

Another Good Opinion—at What Cost?

As a young woman living in New York, ES had been invited to an elegant dinner at the home of a family friend, a member of the European aristocracy who had been sent to England as a young girl and then to the United States to escape the war. The woman lived in an exquisite apartment on the Upper East Side, cultivated white azaleas on her balcony, and prepared elegant dinners. This was definitely a person whose good opinion ES sought. ES tells the story:

"The story begins with the sad fact that I arrived late to one of those elegant repasts, and the meat had been the slightest bit overdone. Nothing, of course, was said, but I felt terrible. About a month later, I had been asked to dinner again and was on my way on the 79th Street bus, crossing to the East Side. Traffic was very heavy, and, in fact, the bus was soon in a traffic jam. I had not allowed sufficient time for unforeseen delays. My anxiety level began to rise and increased even more as the bus completely stopped. I fretted: I can't be late again! What will she think of me? Five minutes later the bus still wasn't moving, and I started fantasizing: If I got off the bus and tried to run, could I get there in time? No. If I got a taxi? No, the taxi would be caught in the same traffic. If I went home I could call her and say . . . what? Anything but admit I had not left enough time again. My need for approval at that moment was 'drowning out the voice of God' and even of sanity.

"At the height of this panic state, I came to some sort of brink of choice and something entirely new—I gave up. I emptied myself of the demand for approval and praise and chose to surrender to the reality of the situation and face the worst: I was going to be late and it was my own fault. Period. And then, standing in that bus in the middle of Manhattan rush hour, the most tremendous feeling of relief fell upon me. The panic symptoms left and I was simply there on the bus between Madison and Park, fallible but free.

"As it turned out I was about fifteen minutes late. My friend accepted my apology graciously, and while the roast chicken was perhaps the tiniest bit less moist and tender than it might have been, we proceeded to have a lovely evening. It's important, as we are tempted to scramble after the approval of others as a substitute for God's love, that we remember we are fallible. For those who feel unkindly toward us, our fallibility may add fuel to their fire; but for our friends, it will be a matter for forgiveness."

It's human and okay to want things, but unless we empty ourselves of the *demanding*, we will never achieve freedom and peace.

The point of emptying a vessel is to provide space for that with which you want to fill it. Empty space is basically neutral, and it can even be dangerous. The natural order abhors a vacuum, and so does the supernatural. Remember what Jesus said about the unclean spirit that went out of a person? When it came back, it found its house "empty, swept, and put in order. Then it goes and brings along seven other spirits more evil than itself, and they enter and live there" (Matthew 12:44-45). If a vessel is emptied, if a space is cleared, then it should in due season be filled with the desired good. If a person makes a clearing in a field to plant a garden, then they should get on with cultivation, or the land will revert to its former state. While we will talk more about filling the vessel in chapter 9, there is one very important point to be made here. Both in gardening and in human spirituality there is a crucial time between the clearing out of the old growth and the planting of new growth. It is a harrowing time. In the dictionary the first definition of "harrow" is "an implement of agriculture . . . to stir the soil," that is, to break up the hard crust and clods.

Another definition states that metaphorically to be "under the harrow" means "to suffer affliction or distress."

In classical spirituality this time is called the spiritual dark night of the senses. It may well begin when a person has realized that "more is better" is a cultural lie, that more stuff or acclaim is not, in fact, providing happiness. That person may start to divest himself or herself of accumulated "stuff," both of material possessions and even of over-reliance on public honors and the good opinion of others. But the knack of inviting spiritual good into that empty space takes time, just as the land, after it has been cleared, must be harrowed and otherwise prepared before it can receive the good seed.

The only choice is to wait it out. But it is very helpful to many people to realize that this decision to move from "stuff" to spirit is a transition, and the transformational stage of "neither still here nor not yet there" is a recognized experience in the spiritual life. Just because it doesn't feel good doesn't mean it's not working. If the intention, the yearning, is for ripeness, wisdom, and freedom in the spirit, they will come in God's time—in due season. And that is the harvest, the quid pro quo. An acorn falls onto the ground and dies—empties itself—and becomes a husk. A caterpillar withers itself into a chrysalis and the chrysalis in turn is emptied in order to free the butterfly. We empty ourselves, die to certain things, *in order to* make room for a more mature stage, a new freedom to live.

CHAPTER FOUR

The Myth of Limitlessness

Myth: "I'll show you how to be a No-Limit person—a winner 100 percent of the time! I can prove to you in very practical day-to-day terms that the only things holding you back from happiness, super health and fulfillment are the limits you impose on yourself!"

—Wayne Dyer, *The Sky's the Limit*

Truth: Each of us has a particular set of skills and talents that by definition limit what we do and where we go. Such limits are among the most important assets we have because they allow us to focus on the particular path that requires our unique skills and to let go of those paths that require skills we do not possess.

Our use of Wayne Dyer's quotation here is not meant as an attack on him. We quote him in this context because the title of his book and his own description of it so clearly reflect the thinking on which so many of us have been raised. Dyer wrote this book in 1980, at a time when the human potential movement had been in full swing for a couple of decades. Those of us raised during this era are acutely familiar with the belief system that suggests anything is possible and the only thing holding us back is—well—ourselves.

In this chapter, we will explore the myth of limitlessness and the huge stress it creates in our lives. We will also explore, as in previous chapters, the spiritual dimensions of this belief and suggest ways to reframe how we view our own limitations.

Family Systems and the Myth of Limitlessness

One of the generations most indoctrinated by the myth of limitlessness is the baby boomer generation. Blessed with unprecedented prosperity during their childhoods in the 1950s and 1960s and further gifted with unprecedented prosperity up to the present, this generation of Americans has been infused with the belief of limitlessness and has on some level experienced the reality of it.

The baby boomers' parents after all had made it through the Depression; they had fought and won several wars; they had, in the aftermath of those wars, built the United States into a world economic power second to none. All of these were legitimate and impressive accomplishments that reinforced the idea that anything is possible if you just put your mind to it.

The definition of what "success" meant growing up back then was quite narrow. The successful kid in the neighborhood was one who excelled at athletics, was a straight A or at least a straight B+ student, was attractive, and had loving parents who catered to his or her every need and want. Going to college was not only expected but also required. The theme was that we were people who had been given tremendous gifts, and we were taught to challenge ourselves to maximize those gifts.

In small towns everywhere, the sky was the limit. It was like Garrison Keillor's Lake Wobegon: where all the men are strong, all the women are beautiful, and all the children are above average. But all the children weren't above average. And those who were merely "normal" in academic or social achievement were at great risk either of becoming workaholics to try to meet the exaggerated expectations of others or of spending the rest of their lives simply feeling like failures.

Expectations were astronomical, and many of the kids never came anywhere close to meeting those expectations. It caused many to blame themselves for their inability to take advantage of the land of limitless opportunity. And for some, that self-blame was more than they could carry and they self-destructed.

Self-blame is one of the most insidious and destructive phenomena humans can experience. The fundamental self-talk is: "I am not good enough" or "I should have done . . ." or "I must . . ." Such self-talk is a manifestation of "limitless thinking." For if, as the belief holds, *anything* and *everything* is possible for *any* individual, then there is really no one to blame other than oneself.

Peer Groups and the Myth of Limitlessness

Juliet Schor wrote an insightful book entitled *The Overspent American: Upscaling, Downshifting, and the New Consumer,* in which she describes how Americans are spending money and acquiring things in order to compete for status within "reference groups." She says that these reference groups change over time but that throughout our lives, we are taught to compete with others in the group by acquiring things. Americans are engaged in a kind of mass overspending, where "large numbers of Americans spend more than they say they would like to . . . more than they realize they are spending and more than is fiscally prudent."

Part of the explanation for this kind of behavior is the belief held deeply by millions that there is no limit to the amount of stuff one should have. If, as Wayne Dyer says, "the sky is the limit" in everything we do, then why not consume unprecedented amounts of stuff? Add to this belief the combination of Schor's point that a lot of the consumption is a competitive response to winning out over one's reference group and the idea that we are finite creatures who yearn for the infinite, and the human engine is bound to be barreling along on overdrive most of the time.

Peer influences exacerbate this phenomenon because the more we seek limitless success and accumulated wealth, the more individuals in our peer or reference group seek to compete by amassing their own wealth. And each step up the ladder is a point of no return because, at least in American culture, there is no path downward, no route down the mountain that is viewed as successful. We are forced through competition and peer influence to keep going, even if the pressure created by such efforts is killing us.

Culture and the Myth of Limitlessness

Lest we think that only the baby boom generation is engaged in no-limit kind of thinking, consider a graduation speech given at a university.

A high percentage of the graduates were young adults in their early twenties, as was the student speaker selected by faculty and fellow students to address those gathered.

The speaker began by talking about how excited she was to be coming up to the podium to receive her diploma. She talked about how her education had been fantastic, but she did feel anxious about the student loans she had built up and the need to find a good, high-paying job and soon. Later in her talk, she described something that happened to her on an exchange trip to Mexico the previous summer. She described how she only had a short time to see things while she was there and she remembers wanting to "see it all." This, she said, was reflective of her generation that wants to do it all, see it all, and have it all in a hurry. She recalled taking a bus out into the countryside to do some sightseeing. When she boarded the bus, the only seat available was the one right behind the driver with a dark-stained glass partition between the seat and the driver, making it impossible for her to see the road ahead. She described it as frustrating since she always liked to see into the future and know what was coming down the road. This seat forced her to look only to the sides as the bus passed through the rural countryside.

On the trip back, she boarded the bus again, and this time she was lucky enough to get a seat on the other side of the bus where she could see the road ahead. But as they were arriving at the town where she was staying, she realized that she had been so engaged in looking down the road that she had missed all the beautiful countryside she had seen when her view of the front was blocked. Her point? In this fast-paced world of seemingly "no-limits," where people want to experience the maximum amount they can, they risk missing the richness of the everyday things. It was a good point—it is the dilemma between the Western view of spirituality (life is a journey) and the Eastern view (life is here, right now, in the present moment).

Our culture glorifies those who have gone the farthest the fastest. Even though we are finite creatures, we get the message that those of us who seemingly defy our finiteness and accomplish feats of limitless proportions will be heroes. Perhaps we feel so confined by our finiteness and so thoroughly yearn for infinite reality that we worship those who seem unfettered by such human limitations.

We also are impacted by the myth of limitlessness in thinking about our careers. We are led to believe that in the land of limitless opportunity we can be and do anything we want, an idea which is not only untrue, but enormously stress-producing. Parker Palmer, author of *Let Your Life Speak*, writes that as a youth, he saw all paths in life as open. None of the various options or "ways" to go were yet closed. Then as he grew older and realized he probably was not going to become a professional baseball player, for example, he would mourn the loss of a "way closing."

But over time, Palmer says he realized that as more and more "ways closing" occurred, his level of stress and anxiety about what to do with his life declined. As it became more and more apparent to him what he clearly could not do, he found he had more time to pursue those few things he knew he was here to pursue. And he didn't spend all his time on one road wondering if the other roads would have been better. He also discovered he did those few things with much greater force and impact.

Think of an image of water running through a hose. When you run water through a hose without a pressure nozzle, it comes out at a slow, even pace. But when you put a spray nozzle on it, thereby covering up most of the opening and forcing the water to travel through a narrow passage, the water comes out with much greater force and impact. So too it happens that when we focus our gifts on those activities for which we seem truly called, we tend to increase in intensity and impact.

The Belief That Anything Is Possible

We are hard-wired for the belief that anything is possible. It's not surprising, then, that we feel ourselves longing to embrace infinity, or to attain limitlessness.

Paradoxically, we get in trouble not because we set our limits too high but because we set them too low. The cultural myth does not promote *true* limitlessness, which is in the dimension of spirit, but rather unrealistic goals (like the sky) which are still finite. The sky's the limit? The sky is not even much of a metaphor anymore for a frontier; after all, we have walked on the moon and explored space. To be captain of the *Enterprise* and travel to worlds unknown seems to affirm our built-in belief that anything is possible, but not even a time-warp leap will satisfy the soul's hunger for the limitlessness that is the spirit's freedom. Neither will imperial power satisfy, nor universal acclaim, nor any lofty attainment in this world or other worlds. But we persist in attaching our desire for the infinite to finite though unrealistic ends. Yearning for what we cannot have is stressful. Even when we get what we think we want, we are often not content.

Maybe a reason that our particular American culture is so filled with the belief that anything is possible is that we have inherited a large dose of pioneer spirit. Many early settlers traveled west to break out of extremely limiting structures, some from literal imprisonment, some from prisons of ideology or caste. The "Westward Ho!" mentality assumed that there was vast, unlimited territory to be conquered and nearly unlimited drive and stamina to conquer it.

America's pioneer spirit is simply a brand of a universal drive. If there is any Everest to be climbed, any record to be broken, any frontier to be exceeded, then human beings have always striven to do so. Witness the Empire State Building, the pyramids, the Colossus of Rhodes, and the realm of Alexander the Great. Not to mention the Tower of Babel, which may be the supreme example of the myth of the sky's the limit. It's evident that human beings are filled with the belief that anything is possible. The catch is that we expect that exceeding physical, spatial, or even intellectual limits will satisfy the soul's capacity for the infinite. It never has.

The Role of Choice

The ability to choose is essential to being human. It is a divine attribute, like the power of love. To be able to choose and to love proclaim that we are created in the image of the Creator. As far as we know, other creatures have instincts that direct their behavior, but only humans seem to have *both* instinct and conscious choice. The faculty of choice is on the one hand our glory and on the other our tragic flaw. With choice comes the freedom to cooperate in our own "ripening," to share in crafting a particular life out of theoretical limitlessness. We can see "way closing," as it is said, and choose fruitfully from among our realistic alternatives.

Alas, this great gift of choice bears with it the inalienable option of choosing poorly. And that has consequences. We can recognize our limits in a helpful way, but we can also limit ourselves to our diminishment by, for example, choosing to drop out of school rather than graduate. We can choose the good, or choose the lesser good, or even choose what we know is evil.

Examples of the consequences go back to the creation myths of many cultures. In the Greek creation story, Prometheus, the Titan, chooses to steal fire from the gods (predominantly a choice for humanity's good); his sister-in-law, Pandora, the first woman, chooses to open the box which contains all the world's ills. In the Judeo-Christian creation story, Adam and Eve choose to disobey the divine limitation on edible fruit. Milton's Satan in *Paradise Lost* says, "Better to reign in Hell than serve in Heaven." Reigning anywhere may *seem* less limiting than serving, but actually, by choosing control over community, Satan is locking himself away from the God "in whose service is perfect freedom."

Fortunately, along with the divine and dangerous gift of choice, human beings have been given a faculty designed to help us choose the good. It is called *conscience*. We can think of conscience in a homey way—as the kibitzer at a game of poker. The kibitzer, for instance, can whisper over your shoulder that it's foolish to draw to an inside straight—the odds in your favor are minuscule. You can then *choose* either to listen and sensibly fold, or to disregard the advice and say to the dealer, "One card, please."

Conscience, which might be described as the capacity for accumulated experience and insight, informed by grace, can grow just as libraries can grow. And, like good libraries, the increase should be qualitative as well as quantitative—there needs to be judicious weeding out. Such cultivation of our conscience is of great importance; in a real sense we become what we choose, and in making our life choices we need all the help we can get.

Sub-myth: Choosing Is Easy

One of the prevalent sub-myths of the myth of limitlessness is that choosing is, or ought to be, easy. Sometimes it is. But sometimes it isn't. It is tempting to put the blame on God for the gift/burden of choice and chafe about how to figure out the will of God for our lives. The fact is, we have been given the gift of choice, and it cannot be returned without loss of our humanity.

An Episcopalian priest is reported to have told the following story on himself. One time he received a call to another parish. The new place offered opportunities for challenging ministry, but he was involved in significant work where he was. He prayed about this choice, trying to see the will of God for his life, but no answer was forthcoming. He consulted with persons he trusted, he weighed the assets of both alternatives, he prayed again, but to no avail: he still had no clear direction. He began to get a little frantic to know the will of God for this next stage of his life. He went into the church and knelt before the altar. He prayed, "God, I want to do your will, but I can't until I know what it is. I'm not getting up from my knees until I have some clarification." And then it came. Quite clearly he was aware of God's answer: "*I don't care* which parish you choose!"

God's grace and the vicissitudes of life notwithstanding, we are left with the lion's share of responsibility for our own decisions. And sometimes making a choice *can* be agonizing. It may or may not be consoling that every mature human being, including Jesus, has had to go through such times. That was what Gethsemane was about. Jesus knew the authorities were out to get him. At supper that Thursday evening, Judas had in some way made it quite clear that he was going to act as informer. Jesus went out to the garden of Gethsemane, where his closest friends proceeded to fall asleep, leaving him alone in the dark. The choice he faced involved staying in Jerusalem, within fatal reach of his strongest enemies or fleeing once again to be able to continue his ministry.

His prayer might have run something like this: "Father, I can't figure out what you have in mind! I've been so sure that your will was for me to bring in the kingdom. But I'm young—not thirty-five yet—it's only been three years since I started my ministry. You know that these friends of mine here, sleeping this hour away, haven't really caught on yet. If I don't escape again *right now*, the authorities will nab me and have me killed. I can't believe that Peter and the others are ready to carry on without me— I'd bet anything that if I'm murdered, they'll be confused and despairing, and if they don't just run away, they'll huddle together in upper rooms behind closed doors for fear of the authorities. Do you really think they can do the work of bringing in the kingdom if I'm gone?" What was he to do? Stay and be killed, or go underground once more and continue to lead the mission? Well, finally the choice he had to make became clear to Jesus, but not before he had sweated blood over it.

If Jesus had to sweat blood over a decision, chances are we may have our moment as well. Freedom of choice is perhaps the greatest gift of human nature, but nobody ever promised it would be a rose garden—or at least a rose garden without thorns.

Sometimes it's too hard to choose well, and despite our best intentions we can't see our way clearly. It is a very difficult and adult process to correctly identify our real alternatives, prioritize them, and take responsibility for our choices. One thing is very important in making choices: not to be so hard on ourselves that we demand certainty before we act. Augustine Baker, a seventeenth-century monk, gives us some excellent advice on this in his great book, *Holy Wisdom:* "In doubtful cases the soul must not expect to obtain absolute certainty . . . an inclination, however slight, toward one side, affords sufficient indication of God's will to be adopted. If there is no perceptible leaning either way, the soul should seek advice or supply the deficiency with her unbiased natural judgment."

It is good to hang in there with the agony of the decision, with the reality of the paradox, the dilemma, until things become clear. We can try to think it out, pray, talk to wise people, and pray some more, but eventually the time comes simply to do one thing or the other.

So far we have gone into the bad news about the human faculty of choice. There is great good news. A novitiate director said, "The will of God is identical with your own deepest desire." The catchword is "deepest," which harks back to our point about discerning intrinsic and extrinsic values in chapter 3.

Another person gave a superb analogy. She had been used to thinking, she said, that trying to find the will of God in making choices for her life was like using a "paint by numbers" kit, filling in little numbered areas on a printed board with correspondingly numbered colors. She tried to figure out what God wanted, and then tried to match her choices and actions to it. One day, however, in a flash of divine insight, she realized that wasn't the way it was at all. It was much more like God giving her a blank canvas and a palette full of colors and saying, "Dear one, paint me a picture!"

Saint Irenaeus said, "The glory of God is a human being fully alive." God's glory—God's will for our lives—is nothing less than the fullness, the richness, of our particular humanity. We don't have to *get* anywhere; we just have to be who we most fully are.

Many people are frustrated by the number of choices they have, and for some it goes beyond frustration. Choice becomes not only frustrating but also intolerable. For many of us the "trouble deciding" is not so extreme, but stressful enough. Part of that stress comes from the pressure of our culture on the individual—there are too many choices, from cereals on the shelf to job ads in the paper.

Facing either too many choices or too few choices can cause major stress. The good news is that discernment is a life-skill that can be learned and acquired. It is possible to practice widening or limiting our perception of alternatives in accordance with the reality of the situation. What needs to be emptied here is the idea that choice should either be limitless or so limited that we virtually have no choice. Learning to choose well not only leads to peace, but to true adulthood and holy wisdom. Meister Eckhart, a Dominican friar (1260-1328), wrote: "Wisdom consists in doing the next thing you have to do, doing it with all your heart, and finding delight in doing it." That kind of wisdom doesn't come cheaply, but it is worth the cost.

Stress often comes from being trapped between contrary messages, messages that may seem contradictory and also equally imperative. The general and cultural message is "Anything and everything is available. You are only limited by the limits you impose on yourself." However, the personal and specific message is too often: "The sky *may* be the limit, but *you*, personally, haven't a chance—you are: (a) not acceptable, (b) stupid, (c) ugly, (d) underprivileged, (e) a born loser." That is, "You can do anything you want to, but you can't really do *anything* right." The effect of these conflicting messages can make a person react like a squirrel in a cage or a rat racing in a maze. There is a need to strive endlessly, while feeling doomed to get nowhere.

To make matters worse, we have conflicting messages not only about pushing limits but also about the faculty of choice. The cultural myth implies that you have limitless choices and that taking advantage of them is effortless—doors will open ahead of you as for royalty on an official visit. Things will fall into your lap or spring out of your laptop. If you do have to make a few choices, like which job to take, which person to marry, or where to go on vacation, such choices should be easy. The opposite, internal message can be that you don't have any choice at all—you are trapped. Then, one can be faced with two alternatives, except both are unacceptable.

The reality to the sub-myth is that choosing isn't easy. It is, rather, a great virtue (from Latin *virtus*, strength). To be a winner in discernment takes as much pain and practice as any Olympic training or martial art. The good news is that, like any great art, it is part gift and part discipline; some people have a natural talent for it, but choosing rightly is a skill that can be acquired and practiced by all. It is possible to learn that there may be another alternative to an apparent dilemma, and it is possible to learn how to prioritize. It is even possible that, though choice may still be difficult, there will come a shift from neurotic anxiety about it to a more existential concern that is not inconsistent with internal peace.

The Shift from Stress to Serenity

There is something we can do to promote this shift from stress to serenity. It is a kind of emptying. We can try not to force decisions, not to "push the river." We can try to empty ourselves of the driven need for immediate answers and control, in order to make space for the wisdom of the spirit—our own spirit and Holy Spirit.

It is in that sort of space where we can pay attention to our dreams. The time between sleep and waking is called the hypnagogic state. Our consciousness is more receptive then, because what Zen calls "busy mind" is not yet, or not still, in full gear. Have you ever been stressed out over a problem or situation and "slept on it," and on waking known clearly what choice must be made or action taken? The point of practicing the art of discernment is to be able to experience that openness and clarity even during our more active hours.

Discernment is a sister of prophecy. Both describe seeing ever more clearly *what is*, recognizing probable consequences, and identifying appropriate action. Perhaps today we use the word "vision" more than "prophecy." Leaders with vision have mastered the art of discernment—of seeing *what is*, and therefore having a better chance at making right choices about how to act from that viewpoint. Well-tuned discernment is not only a gift for leaders but also for those for whom they are authorities and prophets.

Sub-myth: We Aren't Spiritual Enough Yet

Yet another sub-myth under limitlessness exists—if we feel limited in daily life, we just haven't gotten spiritual enough. The myth is that there is no limit—but we feel oppressed by limits, and this is a contradiction. The question from a lot of folks is something like "If God is infinite/limitless, and my spirit (made in God's image) has the capacity for infinity/limitlessness, how does this relate to my feeling so limited in my everyday life?" Is it because I'm not close enough to God? That I'm not spiritually inclined—that I need to work harder at it? It is so easy to forget the great promises of God that we read in the Bible; or even if we remember them, to think that they are meant for other, more "spiritual" people—surely not for me. The prophet Joel hears God say: "Then afterward I will pour out my spirit on all flesh; your sons and your daughters shall prophesy, your old men shall dream dreams, and your young men shall see visions" (2:28). And Jesus says, "But the Advocate, the Holy Spirit, whom the Father will send in my name, will teach you everything, and remind you of all that I have said to you" (John 14:26).

The great promise is that God's Holy Spirit will come to meet my spirit, not after I die, but now, in the now moment. As we stated in the introduction, a definition of the human soul is "the capacity for infinite reality to be held finitely." The mystics of every age and spirituality attest to this; they tell us it is possible to move from believing God to knowing

God. They tell us that we cannot know God with our finite, limited minds, but we can know God in the dimension of love that has no limit. How does this happen? The mystics tell us it is the conjunction of three things: yearning, gift, and the practice of paying attention. First we must yearn, ask, desire to know God in love. Then there is mutual gift—the gift of our truest selves to be open to receive God's promises. Finally there is spiritual practice, such as setting a certain time regularly each day to be still and attentive to God.

Nothing is certain, nothing guaranteed, all is, as in any true love affair, mutual gift. We *are* spiritual enough because God has created us as spiritual beings and has promised God's Holy Spirit of wisdom to meet us and lead us into all truth. If that is what we want! And as we grow and ripen in love, there will be less and less of a difference between being in church or at work; in times of prayer or play or chores. The goal is to know and live in our limits and yet also walk in the confidence of spiritual freedom. Not in certainty—but in confidence: *con fido*, with faith.

If we can hold in creative tension the mystery of the limits of our five senses and our limitless spirit, then the stress of trying to hold together seemingly contradictory realities can be alleviated. Mystery does not oppose everyday reality; it is the medium by which our *dailiness* can be embraced by cosmic or divine reality. It offers us an expanded stage.

Mutuality in Choice

In a sense we each are born to a purpose or purposes. Perhaps we are born with them as the particular acorn is born with the purpose of becoming a particular oak. But how a particular acorn/oak actually turns out is determined by a multitude of internal and external factors: soil nutrients, weather, position among other trees, squirrels, and the logging industry. With human beings another whole dimension is added: the capacity to choose and to participate in the discernment and crafting of our life-purpose. Some people feel they are not up to it and perhaps do better given a clear model to follow. Some put the onus for their purpose in life on the will of God or the whim of the Fates or their guru or the stars. Some go to the opposite extreme of claiming all the responsibility for purpose or lack of purpose, as Shakespeare wrote in *Julius Caesar*: "The fault, dear Brutus, is not in our stars, but in ourselves that we are under-lings." If there is a God, and if God is love, then there needs to be a loving *mutuality* in the discernment and choice. There needs to be cooperation in the discernment of our purpose.

The most important thing to remember about all this is that *our ulti-mate life-purpose is who we are and how we love, not what we do.* Who we are is often enriched by experiences and activities that may seem at the time to be totally extraneous to anything we might have thought would further our life's purpose. As a wit said, "We are created to be human beings, not human doings."

Sub-myth: Busier Is Better

The particular issue of limitless has tied with it the sub-myth of our cul-ture that busier is better. There are roots of this sub-myth in some very early cultures. In the Christian West it has been called the "Martha/Mary syndrome." When Jesus went to these sisters' house for dinner, Martha was busy and, as The New English Bible translates it, "fretting and fuss-ing" about many things. Mary chose to empty herself of distraction and to listen. Jesus named Mary's contemplative presence "the better part."

Through the ages, this little incident has been used to support those people who choose to carry the banner that busier is not necessarily better!

However, it must be noted that there is a great gulf of difference between the contemplation of Mary and "navel gazing." The first is the hard work of listening for and seeking the truth, the second is close to laziness and narcissism. Undoubtedly Mary had her turn at cooking or fetching the water to wash up.

While the busy may see contemplation as passive, in fact contemplation and action are not opposites, they are complementary necessities—like systole and diastole, breathing in and breathing out. Even the Desert Fathers and Mothers preached the necessity of balancing contemplation and solitude with manual work and hospitality.

In American culture, a lot of stress and self-blame, a lot of false guilt, can attach itself to not being busy and competing, or pushing the limits, all the time. How often do you ask someone how they're doing and *don't* get an answer like "busy," "over my head," "swamped," "way behind," or "exhausted"? Often we manage to be proud of being over-busy. The implication is that, despite all, we're making it!

Of course all this stress impacts one's mental health. If early on the compulsion to make it, to push the limits is too strong, and the self-blame for not making it is too painful to bear, a kind of split can take place in one's personality. The lousy and deflated self-image who can't make it is banished to the caves of repression, and the inflated "I can do anything better than you" image is given the place in the sun. That wouldn't be so bad if the klutz image never made itself heard or felt—only, of course, it does. Like any trapped or mistreated creature it can become vicious and aggressive, and, in a desperate attempt to alleviate its suffering, often transfers the blame onto other people and/or external events. This causes mutual hostility and fear. Or the deflated self-image can be expressed in bottomless-pit neediness and all sorts of manipulative behaviors in attempts to get its needs met.

The split, opposite images of klutz and kingpin, are of course both lies, and lying to oneself is detrimental to one's psychological and spiritual health.

Maximizing Our Human Potential

The myth of limitlessness is very different from maximizing our human potential. One thing about all cultural lies—what we are calling myths— is that they are hazy and generalized. Truth is particular and unique. The myth of limitlessness implies vaguely that any child can grow up to be president of the United States, anyone can be Cinderella, anyone can go from rags to riches. For me to maximize my potential, for you to maximize your potential, it is not truth *in general* but my own personal truth, your own personal truth, that we are talking about.

One of the big troubles about myths is that they are so generalized as to be dangerous. In M. Scott Peck's community-building work, the first stage is called "pseudo-community." In this initial stage of group process, one myth or assumption is that we are all nice people, that everyone is pretty much the same. In *true* community, we recognize our differences and hold them in respect. And most often our differences lie in our limitations. To be known for who I really am, to be accepted for where I really am in the hard process of maximizing my potential, is to be free. Individuation, which is another way of talking about maximizing human potential, is hard work. It's not done without pain. It is perhaps the narrow way that leads to life.

It takes costly attention and perseverance to realize our own truth, our extremely particular limitations and our entirely unique endowments.

Only the truth for our own life—*not for yours*—will make us free. And *vice versa*. For example, celibate chastity may be a vehicle for one person to maximize his or her potential, but it might be an obstacle for you to maximize yours. The myth or cultural lie of limitlessness would like to brainwash us into a vague compulsion that we should do it all—or at least get to the top of some unnamed Everest, that we must keep pushing the rock up the mountain like Sisyphus and admit no limitations.

Have we swallowed the propaganda that being limited is bad? Could it be that having limits is good, even wonderful? What, after all, is a limit? Our own skin is a limit and we would be dead without it. Our psychological boundaries are limits, and we would not be healthy without them. The frame around a great painting is a limit, the dimensions of the Globe Theater were a certain kind of limit for Shakespeare, the shores of a great ocean or a small stream are limits.

Our birth and death are the frames, boundaries, and shores—the limits—of our lives. It is the stage, as Shakespeare said, upon which our absolutely distinctive and gloriously delimited life is played out, with all its tragic flaws, to fill its unique human potential. If there is life in eternity, it will perhaps not be limited. But for now, let us glory in our limits because they are what make us splendidly and uniquely ourselves.

CHAPTER FIVE

The Myth of Individualism

Myth: I am solely responsible for my own destiny, captain of my own ship, and master of my own fate. Any reliance on others is a sign of weakness.

Truth: All human beings are interconnected and part of a larger system known as the human species. This species has the paradoxical characteristic of having the capacity to become separate individuals and yet to be dependent on others. It is a predicament.

There is no society on earth that places more emphasis on the importance of individualism than the United States. It is a concept that is so ingrained in us that we almost take it for granted, discounting the need for relationships as a source of essential health and wholeness. Yet we are indeed creatures who need both togetherness and separateness. The question is how to do both in a dualistic, either/or world, and particularly in a culture that places such total emphasis on making it on one's own. This chapter explores the myth and paradox of individualism and attempts to unpack the complicated ways in which we come to embody the belief in doing it all ourselves.

Family Systems and the Myth of Individualism

A woman described what it had been like for her when she and her husband and young daughter lived in Japan. They had very tiny quarters since housing was expensive and space was at a premium. For the first several years, their daughter slept in their bed with them because it was the norm in Japan, not only because of space limitations but also because children were welcome in a family bed. When they moved back to the United States and their daughter was still sleeping in their bed, parents and friends expressed concern that it would psychologically damage the child in some way.

In the United States, we inculcate our young with the myth of individualism almost from the moment of birth. The common ritual is to prepare the baby's room during the mother's pregnancy so that the moment the child is born, he or she can have a separate bed, separate room, separate closet, and so forth.

We buy the young toddler his or her own clothes, his or her own bicycle, a lunch box with his or her name on it. Whereas in many other countries it is common for children to sleep in the parents' bed and feel in the first instant that being a part of the family is more important than establishing one's individual identity, in the United States individual identity is all-important.

We learn that the goal of our existence is to build up an individuated self, a self that has credentials, unique skills, talents, sexual attractiveness, athletic abilities, and so on. Once the self has been nurtured and shaped and established, then we spend huge amounts of time making sure that our separate and unique identity is preserved. All of this takes enormous energy and has the effect of isolating us from others.

Peer Groups and the Myth of Individualism

One of the consequences of our cultural focus on individualism is competition. The call to individuate and become separate entities who must make it on our own is often dependent on beating out the other. If I alone am master of my own fate and others are masters of their own fate, then I am destined to see the other as an "it" at best and as "the enemy" at worst. The myth of individualism precludes our ever moving from "I-it" to "I-Thou" as philosopher Martin Buber described it: seeing the other as a divine act of creation.

Competitiveness is a key component of American culture that we learn from our families—and also from each other. We learn quickly with athletics that there are a limited number who will make the team and the rest are, well . . . out of luck. Collaboration even in team sports is muted by the fact that at the end of the season, the team has a leading scorer, all-star teams, all-state teams, and other measurements that put individual players on a hierarchy. In higher education, some prestigious colleges accept only about 5 percent of all the applicants and the remaining 95 percent are, well . . . out of luck. The effect of all of this is that we see others as competitors, not as collaborators or even brothers and sisters. The idea that we are all interconnected and interdependent is foreign to us.

The fact that we are taught to compete against each other dramatically alters the way we interact. Since we are taught to see the game as one in which there are only a handful of winners and most everyone else loses, we learn to react to others as a threat. It is almost never okay to let down our guard or trust those we are competing against since "my getting what I want is dependent on your not getting what you want." Competition makes us less likely to help our fellow human beings because they become the enemy. No wonder so many more of us no longer trust each other. No wonder so many more of us are living alone and feel a sense of isolation.

Culture and the Myth of Individualism

The idea that we have to make it individually is maybe the single biggest source of stress in our culture. We are continually told that the successful person is the one who individually achieves the greatest feats. And while service or good beyond self, Level Three on our Four Levels of Human Happiness scale (see page 42 in chapter 3) are activities certainly respected by society, the accumulation of *individual* achievement or ego gratification (Level Two) is far more respected and glamorized by the media and the culture.

The reason such reliance on individual achievement causes so much anxiety is because to achieve something literally on one's own is a fallacy.

Even the most brilliant playwright needs help at some things, so does the strongest boxer, the most decorated soldier, the most talented musician, the wisest scholar.

The myth of individualism places enormous pressure on the individual to be good at everything and to be in control in every situation. Because both of these are impossible, we become very good at faking it. We employ a sophisticated series of social masks to give the impression that we are on top of every situation, while secretly we are paralyzed with fear that others will find out the truth. Over half of the chief executives of major U.S. companies name their number one fear as one day people finding out they are incompetent and unqualified to do their job. Apparently, many CEOs have mastered the art of faking it, but in so doing have isolated themselves from others and precluded ever being able to be who they really are.

The effect is for individuals to withdraw further and further into themselves, becoming less open and authentic. Since everyone is wearing the social mask of success and having it all together, we begin to feel we are the only ones who are not all together, and, therefore, we can't let anyone else know the truth.

Irving Yalom, in his classic study of group psychotherapy, has identified curative factors: elements of the group process that improve an individual's sense of health and wholeness (see *The Theory and Practice of Group Psychotherapy*). One of the primary curative factors that group therapy participants report is "universality," the idea that others have the same kinds of problems I do. What is so comforting about seeing others who have the same kind of problems is precisely what is so limiting about the myth of individualism. If we are never allowed to show ourselves to each other as we really are and we get all of our cues about how to be from media images of happy, successful people, then we will come to believe that we are the only souls on earth who are in pain. In short, misery does love company.

The Individual

One definition of "individual" is as follows: a discreet locus of potential consciousness. However, the concept of "individual" deserves a longer look. It comes from a Latin word meaning indivisible, not able to be divided. This is strange, because in almost every culture human beings *have* seen themselves as divided—not only from other individuals but also within themselves. Most often this division has been described as body and spirit, or body, mind, soul and spirit—at any rate, into that which is material and goes back to the earth, and that which is spiritual and may live on in some fashion apart from the body.

On the whole, human nature seems to have known itself as divided, sometimes to the point of internal warfare—what the ancients called "psychomachia": the battle between body and soul. Often this battle is focused on the contrary impulses in human nature to good and to evil. Saint Paul names the struggle that of "flesh" (*sarx*) and "spirit" (*pneuma*). The Greek words refer to those aspects of human nature which are opposed to, and in alignment with, the true God-created self (compare Romans 7:14-25).

The Faustus legend is a classic example of this apparent human duality as the Evil Spirit is whispering to Faustus in one ear and the Good Spirit is whispering opposite advice in the other ear. Hildegard of Bingen in the twelfth century wrote a liturgical drama on the battle for the human soul between Satan and the Virtues. The human creature, far from feeling indivisible, most often feels fragmented. Extreme cases of this are multiple personality disorder and demonic possession. It is very stressful to feel that I *ought* to be unique and integrated, and at the same time feel at odds within myself.

Another way in which humans see themselves divided is into genders—male and female. Not only are there men and women but also there is the feminine element in every man and a masculine aspect of every woman. Many writers, classic and modern, have written of androgyny—the merging of, or desire to merge, both genders in one individual. Coleridge wrote: "The truth is, a great mind must be androgynous." Some writers have suggested that the yearning for the opposite sex is part of a yearning for a disunited human nature to become whole. An example of this from Greek mythology is the story of the blind prophet, Tiresias, who as a result of killing coupling snakes was turned into a woman and lived as one, until seven years later he met two snakes again and was turned back into a man. The inference is that his experience of androgyny contributed significantly to his wisdom of the human condition.

The human individual is not a simple integer, but a complexity of many dimensions and aspects. The feeling of *internal* conflict is intensified by an individual's sense of him/herself in relation to *external* demands. Working out how to relate to others, or worse, *not* working it out, is very stressful. Does an individual have a completely separate existence? The word "existence" comes from the Greek, meaning "to stand out from" (*ex histemi*). And yet we can't stop the world and get off. We are part of the world and the world is part of us. We can't be completely separate, and, except for moments of great enlightenment, we can't be completely one.

Effects of Individualism

The human individual is caught between two primal fears: the fear of being abandoned and the fear of being overwhelmed. In our earliest, most vulnerable state, these are realistic fears of life-threatening proportion: an infant can be deserted, or it can be rolled over on and smothered. Later, although we grow physically less vulnerable, the primal fears may remain or return, especially in moments of stress. So, the first effect, the fear of abandonment, may show up as needy loneliness or a feeling of being marginalized. The second effect, the fear of being overwhelmed, can manifest itself as a fear of being taken over. A person can feel like Atlas holding the world on his shoulder all by himself and in competition with a host of other Atlases trying to grab the world as if it were a beach ball. The stress of competition can make a person feel driven, trampled on, and marginalized. The dilemma here is that the individual is both segregated and racing to keep up or get in front of the pack.

The individual who claims "I can do it all by myself" has to be pretty much on the go all the time. There is little or no time and space to get out of the race, just *to be*—no downtime. The trout stream is one place where one cannot be "got at," where one can have some space just to be oneself. The stream invites the kind of space that allows a person to be just a human being and discover the true difference between isolation and solitude. Isolation implies anxiety or stress about what one is not a part of; solitude implies contentment in one's own chosen time-out.

The third major effect of the myth of the individual after needy loneliness and feeling overwhelmed is the loss of the gift of discipleship. When any reliance on others is a sign of weakness, one cannot be seen sitting at anyone else's feet. Discipleship is a gift because it is an acknowledgment of how human beings learn best. Studies have shown that we learn least well by reading, a little better by hearing, and best by face-to-face contact with persons who are ahead of us on the road of life. Jesus said, "Have you believed because you have seen me? Blessed are those who have not seen and yet have come to believe" (John 20:29). Those of us who have not seen Jesus, or any great teacher, come to believe through the witness of those who have seen.

In almost all other cultures people have not only been willing but also eager to sit at the feet of someone more experienced and usually older. In the Renaissance, an aspiring young artist would become an apprentice in a master's studio and learn by painting cherubs in the corners of the master's works, until the young artist's skill was sufficient to set up a new artist's studio. It was more or less the same in every branch of the arts and crafts. From another culture we have the popularized example of Kung Fu—when the disciple is ready, the pebble is taken from the master's hand. And, of course, in the Star Wars cosmology, there is the rigorous discipleship of training to be a Jedi knight.

In almost every culture except our prevailing one, there are elaborate rituals of discipleship for the young of both sexes that culminate in being received into womanhood and manhood. In our times the myth of individualism has no doubt affected even Jewish Bar Mitzvah and Bas Mitzvah and Christian confirmation so that the element of learning from the elders is minimized and only the celebration is maximized.

One of the best positive examples of modern discipleship was the Frank Lloyd Wright community at Taliesin West, where young, aspiring architects came to sit at the great man's feet. They carried in his firewood and did his other chores so that they could hear his wisdom. Individualism shrinks at that sort of thing. If we must learn something, we will *pay* for it. If we pay for it, the sub-myth runs, we are not indebted and are *not asking for help*. This allows individuals to go to high-tech training programs or to psychiatrists. We are not asking for help or submitting ourselves to somebody else's greater wisdom, we are simply hiring professionals. Which means we are in charge, still in control.

A kind of individualism *à deux* exists in codependency. The two merge into a sort of dyadic entity that isolates itself, does not seek outside help, and often is hostile and corrosive to community. The codependent dyad is typically born out of fear and weakness and only wears a mask of self-sufficiency. There is a great deal of difference between a symbiotic need-iness of this sort and a mature exchange of gifts.

Where individualism prevails, it is not okay to ask for the invaluable insights of wisdom and experience. Individualism robs us of the knowl-edge of our elders and much of the richness of our roots and traditions. In place of our deep truth, individualism offers us a veneer of self-sufficiency. The myth robs us of our human nature as social animals, of our capacity to give and receive gratefully and gracefully; it robs us of community.

Overcoming the Myth

Human beings who live or work together as a group have a tendency to move through phases or stages of interaction. Here we will explore what has to happen for individualism to be traded in for a sense of true community.

An interesting model for the process of leading a group of individu-als into community is one to which we referred earlier, developed by M. Scott Peck. The opening stage in Peck's community-building work is when individuals are brought together in what is referred to as "pseudo-community." At first a group is either too fearful or too com-petitive (or both) to risk expressing real thoughts and feelings. Admission of inadequacy or pain is felt to be unacceptable and so must be either repressed or inhibited. The group's motto at this stage is "No Problem." This, of course, is a lie. Even if a person's life is currently as good as it can get, there is some problem, some limitation, somewhere. There are people at this moment dying on the streets of Calcutta; sooner or later we will all die. Because denial of all problems *is* pseudo, it is not healthy to settle for pseudo-community as a lifestyle, although such superficial pleasantry can be appropriate at a cocktail party or with waiters in a restaurant. Revealing our true selves indiscriminately is not the goal; the goal is to become in ourselves more and more aware of our true nature.

At some point in a group the "No Problem" aspect of individualism usually wears thin and breaks down because, as we noted, the myth doesn't offer much in the way of relating to others except for competition or exclusive twosomes. When the veneer wears thin enough, what we call "chaos" breaks out. Here, people tend to express their feelings of isolation by excluding themselves or others from the group. Or as competition surfaces, they may try to put down or fix others. In either case the group is fragmented into individuals trying to control their environment or exclude themselves from it—either to be captain of the ship, or give up and abandon ship with the rats.

If enough individuals in the group trust the process and stop trying to fix or organize it, the group may move into a stage that we call "emptiness." Emptying is also perhaps the most significant factor in helping people to overcome the myth of individualism.

There are many levels of emptiness—some of which we have discussed in chapter 3. Here are a few more notes on emptiness as it specifically applies to community (deep human connections), as opposed to individualism.

Emptiness is a risky business. It involves giving up the need to control. It consists, among other things, of emptying the "rugged" self-image, what *my* unyielding agenda is, what *I* want to push through. This kind of letting go isn't easy, and it takes a considerable degree of trust. It's risky to trade individualistic control for openness and vulnerability. At the beginning, emptiness often feels like frustration or dejection. But it offers the most effective way to help people overcome the myth of individualism. It means the shedding or emptying of what some people call the false self and others call the ego.

This kind of self-surrender feels like death and in fact it is a kind of death. *But what dies?* Does an acorn die to become an oak? Does a caterpillar die to become a butterfly? "Unless a grain of wheat falls into the earth and dies, it remains just a single grain; but if it dies, it bears much fruit" (John 12:24). Again, what dies? The husk, the chrysalis, the outer coating; we might add, the social mask. These protective shells are no longer needed when the new creature is strong enough to outgrow and naturally shed them.

Consider the lobster. A young lobster develops a hard carapace or shell, which as the lobster grows, becomes too small and must be shed. On the one hand, shedding the shell is the only chance the lobster will have to live and grow; on the other hand, the shell-less lobster is very vulnerable until it grows its new shell and may get eaten by predators. However, if it hangs in there, shell after shell, it will one day become a mature and formidable creature. The point to be made is that the cycle of dying and renewal is both necessary and risky if we are to move toward wholeness.

When the immature husk, the mask, the defense, the shell is cracked open and emptied, new growth, new choices, and new life can emerge. Then a person can have a taste of the stage of true community, where, paradoxically, one is not less individual, but more so. We are no longer either isolated or absorbed—we can relate more consciously and authentically with others.

Two "Strategies" to Live Authentically

Paying Attention: First, there is a discipline that virtually all spiritual paths teach. It has to do with paying attention. One way of putting it is "Wake up! Be there!" This is related to seeing *what is* (not what society and culture says ought to be) and to living fully in the moment. However, being aware is far from easy. In fact, it is a discipline that takes a lifetime of practice. When one has matured or ripened in this art of being conscious, one has emptied oneself of the old spiritual cataracts of isolation and competition and has come into a sense of presence and interconnectedness. Saint Paul uses the word "empty" of Jesus in his letter to the church in Philippi: He "did not regard equality with God as something to be exploited, but emptied himself . . . being born in human likeness" (Philippians 2:6).

In fact, the discipline of dying to the individual self is generally such a long, hard process that we all have to be light-hearted about it sometimes. There is the story of the Zen monk who went up to the street vendor selling hot dogs and said, "Make me one with everything." The vendor did so and the monk gave him a twenty-dollar bill, which the vendor put in his cash box. "Where's my change?" asked the monk. The vendor replied, "Change must come from within."

Though the discipline of awareness, of living the examined life, is difficult and often costly, it is the way both to freedom and to relationship. So one "strategy," for those who are called to it, is to practice paying attention to your life. Who are you, actually and particularly, and what is really going on for you? Far from being navel-gazing or narcissistic, awareness will put us in touch with the reality of others and with our environment. Without self-knowledge there can be no true compassion.

Find a Guide: This leads us to the second tip or "strategy." Because self-awareness is, God only knows why, the less traveled road, it can sometimes get very lonely indeed, and, in fact, there may be a danger of taking a wrong turn, of getting lost. So the second strategy is to find a guide.

Saint John of the Cross pushes the road analogy just about as far as it can go: "Wherefore, upon this road, to enter upon the road is to leave the road; or, to express it better, it is to pass on to the goal and to leave one's own way and to enter upon that which has no way, which is God." Or as Eastern wisdom puts it: "If you see the path in front of you, it is not your path." In these spaces of spiritual nonseeing, individualism fails and one needs a trusty guide.

The traditional name in Western spirituality for such a guide is a spiritual director. You may dislike this term, because it sounds pompous and maybe a bit bossy. We don't want to be directed—told what to do—we want to be listened to and given confirmation that we are on the right track. And indeed, that is the right and proper mode for such a relationship. Here's an example that may help you with the term "director." As you get off the interstate for a meal and you're ready to continue your trip, you find you're totally lost in the small town's industrial district. You drive into a gas station and ask for directions. They tell you, "Turn right out of here, go three stoplights, when you get to the main street with the bus station on the corner turn left, and in about three blocks you'll see the on ramp. If you come to a school on your right, you've gone too far."

The gas station attendants don't tell you where you want to go—you knew where you wanted to go; they helped you figure out how you might get there. They aren't necessarily wiser than you—it is that *they are familiar with the territory.* So also with spiritual directors. If they're worth their salt, they will not tell you where you want to go, much less where you ought to go, but being familiar with the territory of spirituality they can help you keep going there. Pick somebody for a spiritual guide who has been saying his or her prayers for a couple of decades and whose opinion you trust in other areas.

Living with a social mask on all the time is surely a barrier to growth and spiritual health—if not spiritual life. Continuing to be confined in our social mask when we are ready to outgrow it would be like a lobster who wouldn't/couldn't shed its shell. If we feel the call for our spirit to expand beyond the tight carapace of its individualism, then we must risk being open in a new way. That's why it's a good strategy to stay alert and also to listen to someone who has been there and knows the territory. We might even find it's refreshing to be a disciple after all and that learning from others is a really good thing.

CHAPTER SIX

The Myth of Happiness

Myth: The reason we are here on earth is to find eternal, blissful happiness, and once discovered to keep it for our entire life. A corollary principle is that if one is not happy, one must become very good at faking it in order to avoid the judgment of others.

Truth: The reality is that happiness is only one aspect of what it means to lead a fulfilling and meaningful life. Ignoring life's difficulties and pain in order to experience happiness can paradoxically become a barrier to its achievement.

People who have never experienced the process of emptying often ask of the process, "Why do people spend so much time talking about pain? Where does the joy come in? I thought being in community with others meant to be joyful with each other?" These questions are understandable since most of us grow up with the culturally instilled belief that the goal of life is to be happy all the time. The short answer to this question is that often the pain people express when working with others in emptying the myths is something they need to get rid of to clear the way to joy. Our culture does not encourage people to express pain, so when presented with a safe place to do so—like in workshops or with spiritual guides—people can pour it out like an overheated boiler.

In this chapter, we discuss the myth of happiness and how it can be a barrier to true joy. We are not saying one should never be happy. What you will find us closer to saying is that to lead a full life, one must be willing to experience both pain and joy. At best, to experience only the latter and not the former is to limit the experience of both. At worst, attempts to totally avoid pain can result in depression, rage, and even neurosis.

Family Systems and the Myth of Happiness

A professor was asked by one of his students if he thought it was a good idea to have children. The professor, who had four kids, thought about it and then said, "I know a lot of people who have chosen not to have children because they are afraid of the responsibility and the emotional pain it might cause them. I believe children do cause more pain because one exposes oneself so totally by loving so deeply. But kids also bring more joy. On the pain/joy continuum, people with kids get more of both; people who decide not to have kids get *less* of both. It just depends on what one wants."

The decision to have or not have children reflects one manifestation of the myth of happiness: avoid pain at all costs. A couple, seeing the problems some of their friends have had with their children, decide to cut off that entire experience in order to avoid pain.

The pain-avoidance approach is applied to all kinds of situations in our culture. We may decide not to take a new job assignment that involves more risk but also more potential rewards because we make a comfortable living doing what we do now, even though it no longer challenges us. Or we might decide not to commit to a relationship of marriage because it might fail or because we might have to limit our freedom in some other way.

The reality is that the more open one is to experience, the more one experiences both pain and joy. Great thinkers have pointed out that once we know that parts of life are difficult and involve pain, then we can deal with it. It is when the cultural myth claims we can live without pain that we begin to run around looking for ways out of it. The motto comes to mind: "If you can't get out of it, get into it." There is no getting out of pain or joy, so we might as well get into both.

If one of the beliefs or sub-myths of happiness is pain-avoidance, then another one is conflict-avoidance. After all, if I am in conflict, I am not happy, right? The belief in conflict-avoidance, like pain-avoidance, can block one's growth and, more significantly, one's relationships.

For example, many children never see their parents in conflict. It isn't because the parents don't argue but because they want to protect the children from the reality that their relationship occasionally runs into conflict. The idea is to always smooth over conflict, to make things okay, to change the subject when something bad or emotionally painful comes up.

If pain can't be avoided, the cultural myth of happiness tells us to hide the pain, if necessary. A simple story illustrates this: Roger was the older of two brothers. As a young man, he was doing well but his younger brother was struggling with his life. The younger brother had just gotten out of the military and had taken a job first at a fast food restaurant and then as an overworked and underpaid retail clerk in a department store. He was a bit lost. He responded to his struggle by isolating himself from most everyone including his family. Roger's dad was worried and also a bit offended when his younger son did not show up until late in the afternoon on a day he was expected to visit.

Just prior to the brother's expected arrival, his dad, feeling a considerable wave of emotion, ran into the bedroom and could be heard sobbing. When Roger got up to go into the room to see how he was doing, his mother intercepted him, "Don't go in there, your father is not feeling very well." When Roger said he was going to see if he could comfort his father, she responded. "He'll be all right if you just leave him alone for a while."

The message: let people experience their pain behind closed doors, away from the light of scrutiny, alone. Roger's mother was not unconcerned about his father in this situation. In fact, in her own way she was trying to protect him from having others see him in a weak position.

For being in pain means weakness, failure, vulnerability. It means one is failing at individualism. The post-World War II generation especially has bought into the belief that the family must hide weakness and appear happy all the time. It's almost as if the appearance of happiness will attract happiness. There's even the saying, "fake it to make it."

So when our family and friends teach us through modeling that conflict and pain are to be avoided (even if they teach it with the best of intentions), whenever we feel conflict or pain, we learn to repress it. The goal is to look perfect, and happy—to look perfectly happy.

Peer Groups and the Myth of Happiness

One powerful part of the belief system operating here is that we are expected to pretend to be happy even when we are not. This may be one reason why so many people skim along the surface of life, going from one superficial activity to another. Blaise Pascal called life an "endless series of distractions." Maybe it is why we spend billions of dollars watching professional sports. Some people have trouble unhooking the brain. Some unhook by watching baseball; others do crossword puzzles. Still others use drugs and alcohol to unhook. It is not necessarily wrong to look for ways to calm the mind so long as it does not cause physical damage to one's vessel or become a method of completely ignoring what is going on inside. For too many, the latter is the pattern and what is being avoided is the reality that life is not happy all the time.

The general pattern of faking it or "pain-avoidance" is the reason so much depression is surfacing in our culture. For if our culture almost institutionally prohibits the authentic expression of negative or painful emotions, they have to go somewhere—namely, underground. Eventually such repressed emotions will erupt, often at a time and with a ferocity that the individual cannot control. The fact that we all wear the social mask of "having it all together" and of being happy increases the risk that repressed negative emotions will one day erupt with dangerous force. This is especially true for teenagers who are so dependent upon the opinions of peers for self-esteem. What does a teenager do when feeling depressed because his father won't talk to him or because his girlfriend just broke up with him? And as adults, we still carry the same emotions. What do adults do who are feeling an existential crisis of meaning even though by all outward appearances they are highly successful? Do they tell the boss and risk being taken off the fast track because of an inability to handle the pressure? Does the breadwinner tell his or her spouse of plans to quit a six-figure-income job and become a schoolteacher?

Too often, what happens to these people is they simply swallow the pain and grin and bear it and run the risk of implosion. Or, as has been the case with a number of troubled teenagers, explosion. How many stories must we read about "normal" teenagers who one day decide they can't take it anymore and carry loaded weapons to school and begin shooting? When the story is later told, what often emerges is a secretly troubled youth who feigned happiness until provoked with a relatively minor incident that put him or her over the edge.

Culture and the Myth of Happiness

It is not just families and peers who reinforce the myth of happiness. Books like *The Way We Never Were* by Stephanie Coontz document the ethic of the 1950s of sweeping pain and conflict under the carpet. That decade, which was seen as an idyllic postwar boom time, actually had higher levels of teen pregnancy than any decade since, and alcoholism and domestic violence were rampant. We were just very good at hiding these social ills. Books by Norman Vincent Peale and others reinforced this idea of happiness by suggesting we should just "think positively" all the time and our troubles would go away.

But as Carl Jung has pointed out, when we repress negative emotions they do not go away, they just go underground. They become part of the dark or shadow side: "Neurosis is always a substitute for legitimate suffering," Jung said.

The culture encourages us to fake success and happiness even when we clearly are not happy. Interestingly, more and more Hollywood screenplays are addressing this phenomenon. In the movie *American Beauty*, a brilliant but dark satire about suburban American life, Annette Bening plays a real estate agent who publicly wears the mask of happiness and success, but privately lives a miserable life with a poor marriage and a dysfunctional family. At one point, she and her chronically depressed husband attend a business function for local real estate agents. As they are walking into the party, she turns to him and says, "Listen, just do me a favor, act happy tonight." "I am happy, Honey," he says. "No, you're not," she whispers under her breath.

Later in the movie, Bening's character is having lunch with her mentor, "The Real Estate King," whom she is attracted to based on his total embrace of the "fake it to make it" strategy. When he tells her that he is breaking up with his wife, she expresses shock and says, "When I saw you two at the party the other night, you seemed perfectly happy." His response? "Call me crazy, but it is my philosophy that in order to be successful, one must project an image of success at all times."

The "fake it to make it" philosophy is widely practiced in our culture and has its origins as far back as Norman Vincent Peale's *The Power of Positive Thinking*. While positive thinking can actually be a helpful thing, the danger is that one will simply live in denial of the existence of real problems and pain like the characters in *American Beauty*. Eventually, such ignored pain deepens and widens and ultimately can lead to depression.

Choosing to Face Pain and Conflict

People run away from pain and conflict instinctively. Everyone snatches their hand away from a hot stove; all creatures will try to run away from a forest fire. All creatures, including humans, when faced with conflict will experience instinctual feelings of "fight or flight." If we feel we might get the worst of it, we flee. Under certain conditions a creature may *not* run from pain or conflict in order to obtain an extrinsic or greater good. Some animals will risk pain, conflict, and even death to obtain food or to propagate the species. In animals this behavior is as instinctual as the avoidance of pain. It may at times seem bizarre to humans; for example, the salmon killing itself swimming upstream or the male praying mantis being eaten by its mate in the very act of copulation. But unless there is an overriding instinct not to, sensate creatures instinctively avoid suffering and any conflict they are not confident of winning.

However, human beings, made in the image of God, have an innate capacity that can override instinct in any circumstance. We call it free will or choice. And one thing we can choose to do is to face pain or conflict, not just for the purpose of self-preservation or species preservation, but because it most clearly manifests our present truth and because it will nurture our spiritual growth or that of others. We can choose to face and bear pain for love.

In chapter 2 on the Myth of Control, we talked about surrender. What we said there is very important to remember when we are dealing with whether to run from conflict and pain or to stay and risk it for the cause of a greater good. We can't give away what we do not have. We can't take on what we cannot bear. We need to think very carefully, and if we are people of prayer, pray very hard before we choose *not* to run from pain or conflict. It was Jesus who said: "For which of you, intending to build a tower, does not first sit down and estimate the cost . . . Or what king, going out to wage war against another king, will not sit down first and consider whether he is able with ten thousand to oppose the one who comes against him with twenty thousand?" (Luke 14:28-31). If I make myself vulnerable, I need not only to count the cost, but also to be sure of the value of my choice.

A good example of the razor's-edge nature of choosing to face pain and death itself is in T. S. Eliot's play, *Murder in the Cathedral*. Archbishop Thomas Becket is informed that his assassins are waiting in the church to kill him when he comes in. Should he escape by a back door and run away? Or should he do what he always does at this time of day and go into the church to say evening prayer? The question is not whether he will be killed or not—he knows he will be killed if he doesn't run away. The question is, will walking in there be martyrdom or suicide? "The last temptation is the greatest treason: To do the right deed for the wrong reason," Becket says.

This is much the same question that caused Jesus to sweat blood in Gethsemane. To run away or to face the pain? It is also the choice each human being has to make at some time or another. Would this action be heroism or wasteful recklessness? Is this particular avoidance of pain healthy or neurotic? Is this evasion of conflict the peacemaking of the Dalai Lama or is it conciliation covering passive aggression? Is this death laying down my life for my friend or is it Jonestown?

The Goal of Life—To Be Happy?

The Dalai Lama speaks very simply when he suggests that all beings are seeking happiness. It is the purpose of life. Possibly what he means by happiness is what we are calling joy, or blessedness, which is often translated as happiness, as in Jesus' Sermon on the Mount. In fact, you could almost say that Jesus preached the Sermon on the Mount against what we are calling the myth of happiness. Blessed (or happy) are those who mourn? Blessed are those who are persecuted? Notice that to "persecuted" Jesus adds "for righteousness sake." He is not suggesting that persecution in itself is a good thing to choose. He is suggesting that true blessedness does not deny persecution or conflict, but can embrace and transcend them.

On a first level the Dalai Lama's words may sound comforting; on a deeper level they can be disturbing. Both in Jesus' time and now, the happiness myth would have us believe in a simplistic reward and punishment principle: be good and you will be happy; be bad and you will be miserable. Unfortunately when this is turned around we have the myth that if you are happy you must be good, and if you are miserable you must be bad. The temptation is to fake being happy so you can tell yourself you are good, you are okay.

A person looks around and sees that other people seem to be okay, to be happy. Or at least they don't seem to have the secret, unacceptable kind of rotten pain that he or she does. Happiness is presented as deceptively easy to attain. In fact, if we have a sneaking suspicion that we don't have happiness, we feel we *should* have it, and so we tend to convince ourselves and others that we *are* happy—in other words, we fake it.

Each person may have a slightly different reason for faking it. When you were a kid (or maybe you will recognize this as something you've said as a parent), if you weren't happy, if you were sad or angry, your mother might say something like: "Pull yourself together. I'm not going to talk to you when you're like this—come back when you've stopped crying." So not being happy, or at least not acting happy, essentially meant to be abandoned. Children learn early to fake being happy to avoid that "abandonment" or nonacceptance. Some of us may reach adulthood before we realize what real conflict feels like.

This issue of faking it is not a simple one. There are at least two ways we can look at it. The first is denial of pain and conflict, which means succumbing to the cultural lie. The second is in the sense, "Fake it to make it."

A word is necessary here about the fact that it is possible to "pretend" to be happy in the sense of *practicing* or *preparing* to be happy. If, for example, you are angry at something that has been said to you, and yet you manage to respond with gentleness, that's not pretense or hypocrisy. That means you have been practicing gentleness, and although the feeling of gentleness isn't perhaps as readily available in the moment as the feeling of anger, it is there in you, waiting to be called up and used.

A kind of assumption of happiness can only be done when we don't lie to ourselves. *First* there is a need to recognize the sadness or pain. I am hurt. I am angry. I am depressed. *Then*, without denying that knowledge, one can try to practice happiness. Sound impossible? People have told me of various ways they have found to practice happiness in the midst of depression. One example is in music, something like Bach's *Concerto for Two Violins in E Major*. The second movement in particular may seem the saddest piece of music in the world, and Bach seems like the only human consciousness able to reach down to the place of sadness where we are and be there with us. As we feel our pain met and acknowledged in this way, we are then ready for the third movement, which is brighter and lighter. It helps us practice happiness, in the best sense of "fake it to make it," and pick ourselves up and get on with life.

So pretending in the sense of lying to oneself won't work, but exploring what happiness might be for you, even when you know you have cause for unhappiness, can be good practice for learning how to open up to joy. And that *is* the purpose of life.

What Does God Think about Happiness?

We don't pretend to know what God thinks about anything. We can talk and write about what we think God thinks, as long as we realize that all our theology is finally taken into mystery and that it would be easier for Hamlet to understand the mind of Shakespeare than for us to understand the mind of God. So, all disclaimers notwithstanding, we trust the spirit of wisdom and truth to speak to us through scripture. We can glean some hints about what God thinks about the whole idea of being happy.

The fifty-third chapter of the book of Isaiah, where we find the description of The Suffering Servant is a poetic antithesis of the happiness myth. The cruelly disfigured servant who will be exalted by God is taken by scholars as meant to be Israel and has been adopted by Christian writers as a prefiguring of Christ. "He was despised and rejected by others; a man of suffering and acquainted with infirmity" (53:3). This is the man (or people) whom God will exalt and lift up. It is clear that God does not expect us or particularly want us to be serenely happy all the time in this life. God's chosen servant, God's chosen people, God's most beloved son, are characterized as miserable. God is truth; God calls us to *be real*. It is our faithfulness to our reality, no matter how harsh, grief-stricken, or even unjust it may be, that God will reward with compassion and exalt.

And what about Job? This great work certainly deals with the doctrine that righteousness *should* bring happiness and prosperity, that wickedness *should* bring unhappiness and misfortune, and that obviously this is not always the case. While this is not the place to analyze the subtleties of the purpose and teachings of the book of Job, the point is that humanity has always been plagued by the idea that if you are good, you should be rewarded by being happy, and if you are bad, you should be punished. Perhaps consequences of reward or punishment for being good or bad are passed down from parent to child, as the infant is toilet trained and generally civilized.

Inevitably there comes a time when one is punished when one *hasn't* been bad, or has gotten away with a bad act that has not been punished. Where is parental justice? It is natural that we first see God as Parent. Where is Divine Justice? Why are good people not always rewarded by happiness, and why do some bad people get away with murder? On the first and rational level there is no answer. Unfairness happens. But there is one important thing to remember. The "happiness" that can come to the "wicked" (as when we see such a person wielding great power and "spreading . . . like a green bay tree" [Psalm 37:35 KJV]) is not true joy. Good fortune is not necessarily identical with good cheer. Think of the famous who seem to have it all—looks, riches, talent, popularity—and yet have died from drugs and/or alcohol. Were they *joyful?* Just as things will not necessarily make us happy, so also with behaviors. There is nothing we can *do* to assure happiness.

Some human beings have focused on trying to overcome or discount pain by becoming indifferent to it. The trouble with this approach, sometimes referred to as stoicism, is that if you become indifferent to pain, you run the risk of also becoming indifferent to delight. One's ability to experience joy is directly linked to one's ability to experience pain.

There may be two dead-end roads in this matter of striving for happiness. One way that will not get us very far is refusing to move beyond the stage of bitter rage at pain and injustice. It may be appropriate to be angry *at first*, even angry with God, but eventually we do well to stop shooting ourselves up with adrenaline and take the turn toward reconciliation and peace. The other dead-end road is to give up and become a compliant victim of our pain. The alternative to strive for is to look to the larger picture and find the glory at the heart of reality.

Playing the "Bum" Hand

When you play cards, you are happy when dealt good cards and generally unhappy with bad cards. Some players, however, enjoy every hand—good or bad. When they get good cards, they are happy in the usual sense of the word, but when they get a "bum" hand, they are not unhappy in the usual sense because it presents them with a challenge. They can show that they are really good players because they can play a bad hand just as well as a good one. And overall, these people really enjoy the game. This is what we should strive for in life. In the larger picture, over the long haul, or as the theologians say, *sub specie aeternitatis* (under the aspect of eternity), life is a splendid adventure and challenge, and we can learn to play even the "bum" hands with greater skill and enjoyment.

It may be that the Holy Trinity contains within itself the mystery of suffering and joy. God the Father-Mother is the glory; God the Son, Jesus, is the suffering and the passion, God the Holy Spirit is the *dailiness*. The dailiness may be the hardest to grasp—but the delight of each moment— playing whatever is in your hand—is the true answer to the human yearning for happiness.

There is some truth in the myth of happiness, as there is in all myths. The purpose of life *is* to find happiness, or as Joseph Campbell put in *The Power of Myth*, to follow (and find) our bliss. The trouble is, we don't have a very clear idea of what or where happiness will be when we find it—and we haven't a clue what to do with the unhappiness we encounter on the way. Tragedy, pain, injustice—they just don't fit in.

We are plagued by the question that has haunted humanity down the centuries, and which brings us back to why we have constructed the myth of happiness. Why pain? What is the purpose of suffering? Our response is what you might call "How to get from suffering to glory in five not-so-easy lessons": the purpose of suffering is wisdom, the purpose of wisdom is freedom, the purpose of freedom is compassion, the purpose of compassion is love, the purpose of love is glory.

CHAPTER SEVEN

The Myth of Being Good

Myth: The most important thing we can do is to be good and do good things as prescribed by a specific set of moral codes.

Truth: The most important thing we can do is to become increasingly aware and accepting of our nature: our nature in relation to God, in relation to ourselves, and in relation to each other.

The myth of perfection is about images in the culture which suggest we need to perform perfectly and has more to do with "doing." The myth of being good is more about who we are and has more to do with "being." It is the message that says we have to *be* morally good all the time and if we are not, we need to walk on our hands and knees for a thousand miles repenting.

In this chapter, we will discuss good and evil, the role society plays in our definitions of them and the link between doing and being good. We will also discuss two important conditions that are related to the myth of being good: guilt and shame.

Family Systems and the Myth of Being Good

Looking at childhood, we see common issues: a lot of activity engaged in is to cover up a feeling of not being good enough, not measuring up. Expectations are not only that we should be good at activities like school and athletics but also that we should be morally good. Since evil and immoral thoughts happen, this creates real angst. But as the individual looks around and everyone seems to be "on board"; they have agreed to "get with the program." The "program" is to look like we have it all together all of the time. The pressure both to *do* good and *be* good is enormous.

For many people, the issue of being good is associated with nothing less than salvation: you will not get to heaven unless you "straighten up and fly right."

There is a huge segment of the population that apparently views God as a judge. Studies conducted by the Roper Center for Public Opinion ask a cross section of the population each year to describe their image of God on a scale of one to seven, with one being God as "judge" and seven being

God as "lover." Each year, an average of 37 percent of respondents say they view God as "judge" and only 8 percent say they view God as "lover." This is significant because if four of ten people see God as a judge, and if we are made in the image of God, then it should not be surprising that many of us judge ourselves and others harshly.

Imaging God as judge is not so much a question of right or wrong as it is a developmental issue. A child is not necessarily wrong in seeing a parent as dispenser of rules, rewards, and punishments; and an adult is not necessarily right in moving beyond rules and laws. Also, it is a necessary and a very good thing to have judges in this world, and there can be very holy judges. To the people of the First Covenant, the law and justice and righteous judges were very important. And they still are to all of us today. There is nothing wrong with seeing God as a righteous judge.

But humanity is called beyond only living by law to being mature lovers. We are called beyond Level Two Love, which is justice, to Level Three Love, which is mutual gift. We are made in the image of God, and as we become more capable of mature love, we are able to image God as the ultimate mature lover—as perfect, complete love itself. When this happens, it may naturally take precedence over less mature or less ripened imaging. Since no individual or group or nation functions on any of the three levels all the time, it is good to have judges and nurturers as well as friends and lovers. Jesus said, "Do not think that I have come to abolish the law or the prophets; I have come not to abolish but to fulfill" (Matthew 5:17). Jesus does call us to be friends. It can be very bad news to image God only and permanently as a severe (not to say unjust) judge. We may not need to abolish that image, but we need to develop others.

Our sense of self-blame or shame comes from the fact that everyone around us seems to look so together. A primary reason why we pretend to have it together is to avoid judgment. It is important for us in our family systems to affirm that it is okay to *be* the way we are, even if we have impulses that seem socially unacceptable.

Labels of "good" and "bad" are placed on what is most often simply human nature. In the quest to avoid being bad, we often retreat into our own worlds out of fear that someone will discover how bad we are. We are not saying that "anything goes" in terms of one's behavior. Many post-modernist thinkers argue that since everything is relative and based on perception, it is okay for humans to do anything they want. The fact is there are moral codes and systems of conduct that, if followed, can lead to a more fulfilling and complete life. Conversely, there are systems of conduct that can lead to a disastrous life. C. S. Lewis addressed this point in *Mere Christianity*:

> People often think of Christian morality as a kind of bargain in which God says, 'If you keep a lot of rules, I'll reward you, and if you don't, I'll do the other thing.' I do not think that is the best way of looking at it. I would much rather say that every time you make a choice, you are turning the central part of you, the part of you that chooses, into something a little different from what it was before. And taking your life as a whole, with all your innumerable choices, all your life long you are slowly turning this central thing into a heavenly creature or into a hellish creature: either into a creature that is in harmony with God, with other creatures, and with itself, or else into one that is in a state of war and hatred with God, and with its fellow creatures, and with itself. To be the one kind of creature is heaven: that is, it is joy and peace and knowledge and power. To be the other means madness, horror, idiocy, rage, impotence, and eternal loneliness. Each of us at each moment is progressing to the one state or the other.

Lewis's image can serve as a kind of barometer for individual choices we make in our family life. When confronted with how to respond to a screaming child or an angry spouse, we can ask ourselves, "What response can I choose that will move us in the direction of becoming heavenly creatures?"

Peer Groups and the Myth of Being Good

M. Scott Peck had an interesting idea about how everyone has a murderer inside. Each one of us has one kept in a fairly well appointed jail cell, with a big padlock on it. Peck described how he fed his murderer every so often and took good care of it because he wanted to be able to consult with it from time to time. He said there are things he could learn from that dark part of himself.

The idea is that the human organism is capable of doing every kind of behavior that has ever been done, good and bad. The best way to ensure that the murderer and other characters that represent undesirable behavior stay locked away is to acknowledge their existence, to accept the reality of the whole of our self. If evil remains in the dark, shadowy byways of the unconscious, it gets thicker and darker, more unpredictable and also more uncontrollable.

The problem is that our culture does not allow human beings to acknowledge these dark byways. This lack of acceptance for the unacceptable is nowhere more prevalent than among teenagers who are all looking for validation. More and more, their validation seems to come not from compliments from each other but by winning the contest to shame and ridicule each other. It is a defense against the onslaught of shaming criticism: your best defense is a good offense.

The effect this has is to make it absolutely impossible for kids to talk to each other in any kind of nurturing, accepting way. Street talk that teases, shames, and ridicules makes it less and less likely that human beings will get to the point where they will be able to accept each other and possibly even reveal some of the things about themselves that are not very good. Such talk ensures that the social masks will stay on, the defenses will remain up, and the parts of all of us that are "bad" will remain hidden from view where they can do the most damage.

What would happen if the public school system had a day set aside each year called "no teasing/no kidding" day? How would the average junior high school student's day be different if on just one day, no one in the entire school was allowed to tease him or her? How would the over-weight thirteen-year-old feel about going to school? How would the pimple-faced fourteen-year-old feel? How would the shortest kid in the school feel? How would the tallest kid feel?

Human beings are diminished by arbitrary judging, by this tremendous peer action. Who really loses at the twenty-year class reunion when the talk is of the homecoming queen's weight gain or the balding of the foot-ball quarterback? Judgment of one another and of ourselves for falling short of arbitrary standards does not move us in the direction of wholeness.

Culture and the Myth of Being Good

One way the myth of being good shows up in our culture is in how we treat public figures who have committed sins or engaged in bad behavior. The politician who has taken a bribe or committed adultery realizes that if such behavior ever becomes public, he or she will be labeled as a "sin-ner" and might never recover. When this politician runs for reelection, the airwaves will be filled with negative ads reminding the public of the sinful behavior. The cultural message this sends is (a) you should never do anything bad, and (b) if you do something bad even once, it is likely to be permanent.

There is a growing body of research that suggests that how we explain our own behavior to ourselves, whether we have an optimistic or pes-simistic "explanatory style," is a crucial determinant of mental health.

Researcher Martin Seligman says pessimistic explanatory style is when you make a mistake and you explain it as personal (it's all my fault), permanent (it's always going to be like this), and pervasive (it will affect everything I do). Optimistic explanatory style is when you interpret a mistake or bad event as not personal, not permanent, and not pervasive. Unfortunately, our culture tends to encourage the former and discourage the latter.

So if we should accept ourselves as we are and try to empty ourselves of negative beliefs, does this mean we should not try to be good? And if we should try, to which set of moral values do we subscribe? Should we follow the creed of the Boy Scouts to be trustworthy, loyal, helpful, friendly, courteous, kind, obedient, cheerful, thrifty, brave, clean, and reverent?

Some of these beliefs make a lot of sense and would probably constitute good news. But what if I can't always be cheerful or kind? What if there are days when I am clearly not brave or friendly? We need a set of moral guidelines for how to move toward positive beliefs. But, if I look at them as absolute states or dualities, where I either am or am not kind or courteous all the time, then I will be asking for self-blame and shame.

One alternative is to choose to see beliefs and values as different manifestations of the same reality or as being on a continuum along which we are moving. Viewed this way, we can simply check our progress based upon the direction we are going rather than whether we have arrived. This alternative view would not only allow us to exercise more self-compassion but would also mean living closer to truth, which means freedom.

Choosing the Good

The question that follows logically is, "Then why should I or anyone take the hard road of trying to choose the good?" Some people do seem to take advantage of the principle of unconditional love and defend their unacceptable behavior by saying, "You need to accept me just the way I am." It is all very well to say, "Love the sinner and hate the sin," but it is not always so easy to do. Especially if a person who acts violently or abusively claims, "How I act is part of who I am." Such people need to be told in love, "I accept you, but what you are doing to yourself and others is not acceptable." To love them does not necessarily mean to vote for them, to put them in power, or to put weapons—material or verbal—at their disposal. To love them may mean, in extreme cases, to lock them up.

The next question might be: "Even if I can accept this person as they are—should I?" This leads us into the more complex aspect of the issue. Even if God *can* accept us or others no matter what we do (after all, God is all-mighty) *ought* God to accept badness? (God is all-goodness.)

The ancient theologians came up with a formulation that states that God has two wills: God's will of good pleasure and God's will of permission. This echoes in a sense the distinction we made earlier in talking about surrender: to accept a bad thing is not necessarily to condone it. God does not condone or take pleasure in evil; God accepts the reality that God permits. Of course the next question we can ask is, "If it is not God's *good pleasure*, why does God *permit* evil?" The final answer to that is that we don't know; the ancient theologians called this whole problem the mystery of iniquity.

But this mystery may have something to do with the nature of love. (God is love.) To be worth anything at all, love must be freely given. If love is demanded or imposed, it comes close to manipulation or rape. Mature love is the free and chosen mutual gift of two independent persons. In order to be free to choose to love God and to love the good, there must be a real alternative. We must *really* be free to choose the lesser good, to choose away from love, to choose evil. Only the freedom of that decision gives our option for love its value.

There is another dimension to this complexity. We might ask: "How much free choice did someone like an Adolph Hitler really have?" To what extent were the cards stacked against him by nature or nurture or both? What about children—even infants—who are so damaged and traumatized, so inhumanely treated by parents and/or peers that they have little motivational recourse beyond the animal instincts for survival and domination? We read, for instance, that Hitler was brutalized by his father. This opens the discussion of how much choice there is in every evil act and how much force of circumstance—how many childhood scars contribute to evil?

Another way to put it is to speak of positive and negative programming. What is the ratio in any given human being between negative programming and the freedom to choose? When we come down to it, we must ask how much of our own behavior is shaped by nature and nurture; what models for good choice have we had? How much grace have we been given? God only knows how well we have done with what we have been given. Jesus said, "The one to whom much has been entrusted, even more will be demanded" (Luke 12:48).

When it comes to self-judgment, perhaps all we can do is commit ourselves to a continual discernment of the gifts we have been given so that we may extend ourselves in understanding, choosing, and acting for the good. Think of an analogy with Pharaoh and the Hebrews in Egypt. Pharaoh, he of the hard heart, ordered that the Israelites should make bricks without straw. If, for all our discerning, we cannot finally know how much straw (grace, and/or lack of negative programming) we have at any given time, then we cannot, without being as hard-hearted to ourselves as Pharaoh, demand of ourselves such and such a level of goodness.

But part of the mystery is that we can, in cooperation with grace, learn how to be conscious, grow in discernment, and learn better how to choose the good. Perhaps the only reason for accepting people as they are, regardless of what they do, is to create an atmosphere where they can take the risk of trying to be different and choose better. Not only can God's grace help us with this transforming process but also we can help one another. Acceptance, withholding judgment, makes possible the movement from compulsion to choice: the way to mature humanity.

Good Works

Is there truth to the idea that the more we do for others, the greater our chance of going to heaven or of being with God? Before we go into the question of good works, let's talk a little about what heaven could mean. The usual concept of heaven has a lot to do with what we talked about in the last chapter—freedom from all suffering, happiness, joy, bliss. This holds true in many spiritual traditions. Celebration, feasting, and banqueting are frequent components or symbols of paradise.

In the Christian tradition a splendid image of heaven is found in Revelation 19:9 where we read: "Blessed are those who are invited to the marriage supper of the Lamb." Celebration, music, feasting, joy—in honor of what? Of the consummation of love in sexual union! This is, of course, an analogy—but what a brilliant analogy—of the blissful union of Christ and his Bride: the Bride being that part of humanity who choose to join with him in love.

Some sections of Christianity have gotten off the track around this issue of joyful celebration. They seem to have forgotten a lot about Jesus' party stories. For instance, overlooking the fact that everyone is invited from all the highways and byways, they start considering merit and qualifications, as if you could only get in if you could afford the cost of five hundred good works per plate. There is a lot about dinners and festive meals in the New Testament, and they seem to be not only "Come one, come all" parties, but "Come as you are" parties. You don't have to be respectable, or even good, to be included. You can be a notorious sinner and be more welcomed as a guest at the dinner party than the righteous-seeming host.

There is one notable and disturbing exception in the New Testament: the story of the wedding feast where one guest came without a wedding garment and was rejected. The question here is, "What does the wedding garment signify?" The Puritan and juridical elements of Christianity would probably conclude that the wedding garment indicates good works and clean living, not to mention temperance and severity of lifestyle, but everything else Jesus ever said or did would seem to speak against this interpretation. "John the Baptist has come eating no bread and drinking no wine, and you say, 'He has a demon'; the Son of Man has come eating and drinking, and you say, 'Look, a glutton and a drunkard, a friend of tax collectors and sinners!'" (Luke 7:33). What if the wedding garment stood, rather, for a commitment to maturing in love, and a yearning to be with God. What if the wedding garment in that context meant a growing capacity for joy?

It is not that good works are not important. The point is that, like any love-gift, they need to be given with no strings attached. A good tree produces good fruit. A full, mature human being, a human being fully alive, will produce good works. And not out of a sense of grim duty, such as is indicated by the Protestant work ethic. On the contrary, God loves a cheerful giver. When a gift, a good work, is given out of cheer, out of joy—out of one's very goodness of being—then it's a love-gift, and that kind of cheerfulness is also good practice for the heavenly celebration.

Being "Bad"

The Greek word most frequently translated as sin in the New Testament is *hamartia,* which originally meant missing a mark or a target. When applied to moral things the idea is similar; it is missing the true end of life. Sin is a deliberate choice of the lesser good or the downright bad. Sin is a choice away from love and against one's conscience. One dictionary mentions "a deliberate violation of a religious or moral principle." There must be the element of deliberation or choice for it to be sin. For instance, when the hierarchy at Rome excommunicated Martin Luther, it did not convict him of *sin.* The Roman Church at the time could not contain Luther and his teachings within its communion because Luther's beliefs, actions, and writings were too divergent from its norms. The church could proclaim him a heretic, but not a sinner, because it could not establish that Luther had acted against his conscience.

What exactly does a deliberate or conscious choice mean? How conscious is conscious? What may help answer that is what we call the Continuum of Inadvertence. By that we mean that there may be degrees of consciousness behind any sin, any particular choice for the lesser good.

Here's a very simple example at the inadvertent end of the continuum. Say you are visiting someone's house overnight. Before saying goodnight, the hostess tells you how to turn on the coffeemaker in the morning if you awake before she does and where the milk is in the refrigerator. So the next morning in due course you open the refrigerator and see this gorgeous baked ham ready to be heated up for Sunday dinner. And there is a little crispy, delicious-looking bit sticking out on one end. Before you know it—it is down your throat. Did you do something wrong—something like gluttony or maybe even stealing? Did you make a conscious choice to swallow that tidbit? How conscious? Could your choice of action be called deliberate? Is it just inadvertent?

On the other end of the spectrum is the kind of premeditated decision that runs something like this: "My supposed friend broke my confidence; I'm going to teach her a lesson, make her feel as bad as I do. As soon as I get a chance, I will." The conscious intent of most of what we call sin is somewhere between the two extremes of the continuum. Only God knows exactly how deliberate each choice was, and how much instinct, negative programming, and circumstances influenced it. All we can own and confess to is our willful consent, whatever part of the whole picture that may be. In addition, we can resolve to continue to inform and follow our conscience.

When it comes to sin, the impulse to negate badness, to sweep it under the rug, can have profound implications. Both sins that we have committed and those that have been committed against us can be covered up so deeply that we are no longer aware of them at all; this is called *repression*. The next strata up toward consciousness we call *inhibition:* those bad things that we could remember, but we don't want to, or choose not to think about. Close to this is *self-deception* or *denial*—the bad thing is available to our consciousness, but we say "it shouldn't be" so convincingly to ourselves that "shouldn't be" becomes "can't be, is not." An example of this is the anecdote about the 79th Street bus (in chapter 3), that one cannot possibly be a person who is late for a dinner engagement *twice!* Denial to oneself or others can be self-defense, or it can move to downright lying. The big trouble with lying is that it traps us in unreality.

We have talked about awareness and how essential it is for spiritual growth. In talking about badness and sin, it becomes clear how hard and often painful awareness can be. It isn't easy to empty ourselves of the will to repress, inhibit, deny, cover up, and generally not acknowledge our faults, mistakes, and perhaps especially our sins—sins being those bad things to which we, at least to some degree, have consented.

The Seven Classical Sins

Not many people in our culture talk about sin anymore, maybe because a rather morbid attitude toward sin prevailed in parts of the church in the last few centuries. Ignoring sin seemed to be a healthy corrective to a tendency to over-stress our sinful nature. However, it is undeniable that people do know themselves capable, and culpable, of choosing against the good.

Sin is trying to take a shortcut to joy. The trouble with this apparent shortcut is that it doesn't really get us where we most deeply want to go; on the contrary, it often lands us, like it did Bunyan's Pilgrim, in the Slough of Despond.

Pride

Let's first take a look at pride. Today the sin of pride might be seen as narcissism, ego-inflation, or self-aggrandizement. We are tempted to think it will win us self-esteem or "perfection."

There is, of course a good kind of pride, such as taking pride in our work. Pride, in the sense of healthy self-esteem, is identical to true humility. It is seeing ourselves as we really are. The pride that is sin once had the name of "vainglory" which is quite appropriate: glory that is in vain, which is a lie. A poor self-image is the flip side of vainglory; both are the opposite of true humility. People tend to have flip images of themselves: a miserable image and an inflated image. Neither is accurate. They are both distorted like reflections in a fun house, where we move slightly and look much fatter or much thinner than we really are. True humility, which comes by way of careful self-knowledge, includes all the parts and images of ourselves, the bestial as well as the noble. We get true humility through the hard work of self-knowledge and self-acceptance. One of the loveliest descriptions of humility is by Anthony Bloom in his book, *Beginning to Pray:*

> The word 'humility' comes from the Latin word '*humus*' which means fertile ground. To me, humility is not what we often make of it: the sheepish way of trying to imagine that we are the worst of all and trying to convince others that our artificial ways of behaving show that we are aware of that. Humility is the situation of the earth. The earth is always there . . . somewhere we cast and pour out all the refuse, all we don't need. It's there, silent and accepting everything and in a miraculous way making out of all the refuse new richness in spite of corruption, transforming corruption itself into a power of life and a new possibility of creativeness.

The right way to get this "new possibility of creativeness" is by the hard way of self-knowledge and self-acceptance.

Avarice

Perhaps the "besetting sin" of our society is greed, or what used to be called avarice. A "besetting sin" describes the situation when one pattern of shortcutting predominates. For instance, when the pressure is on, do you tend to place yourself above such things (that would be pride), go on a shopping binge (greed), gripe about how other people have all the luck (envy), turn on the TV or oversleep (sloth), find a sexual outlet (lust), go to the refrigerator (gluttony), or chew someone out (anger)?

It does seem, as we suggest in the chapter on the myth of accumulation, that our culture's shortcut of choice may be greed. Avarice does not know the meaning of gift. Its characteristics are acquisition, exploitation, and consumerism. The temptation is that by accumulating more and more things we will find security, invulnerability, and ease. As we have discussed, this is a myth or a lie. The only way to come to true ease of mind and spirit is to empty ourselves of the demand for security and sufficiency and instead nurture the capacities of trust and gift.

Envy

If greed or avarice is grabbing what we can get, envy is hankering after what we can't get. (If the object of envy becomes attainable, the sinful attitude toward it might shift to greed.) The lie that envy is based on—its temptation—is that if we could only have what we don't have, or be what we are not, we would be okay. Part of the lie of envy is that we *can* have it—we can get it, whatever we envy—and then we will be happy and good.

One of the offspring of envy is judgmentalism. It is common to condemn or "put down" what we envy in others in hopes that we can feel better about our own impoverishment. Envy is an attempt to shortcut the hard work of accepting ourselves as we are, with what we have been given, and trusting our own okay-ness and indeed our unique worth.

Lust

Lust is another of those words that we use to describe a healthy condition as well as the sin. It is fine to have a lusty appetite either for food or for sex. What the classical sin looks like today is when we distort the natural instinct in order to serve the lie. The lie is that having more and better sex will bring us happiness, or at least the forgetting of all trouble; we will find release, and/or affirmation, and fill our soul's hunger to be loved.

A man who has a Don Juan-kind of sexual addiction best illustrates this. It's a dreadful disease that robs the man's life of commitment and his spirit of peace. He can't enter into conversation with one woman without casting an eye around the room for the next. Consequently his lust is never satisfied: he can never enjoy the woman he is with because he is always on the lookout for someone else. We are reminded of Dante's image of damned souls driven by lust in the Second Circle of Hell: "Here, there, up, down, they whirl and, whirling strain / with never a hope of hope to comfort them / not of release, but even less of pain."

Being blown around by a dry hot wind is a fitting image for the victim of sexual addiction and what has been called the *Playboy* mentality of sex. The pursuit promises fulfillment, but the promise is a lie. All is wind, all is vanity.

The true way to sexual fulfillment involves ripening in the three levels of love we spoke of earlier in chapter 1 (narcissism, justice, gift), so we see a sexual partner as truly other, so we can move from driven compulsion to mutual gift. As that happens, we are more able to risk our true selves and move to what Martin Buber calls a "I to Thou" relationship, a sharing of intimacy.

This maturing also makes commitment possible. An analogy is with wine. If you want a vintage wine, you have to begin with good grapes. But then you trample on them, put them together in a cask—a dark, still place—for a long time. In that confinement a lot of change takes place, of fermentation and aging. Grapes are good, but if you want wine, you have to go through all that to get it. A committed relationship and the maturity that allows intimacy take time and caring attention. And "hanging in there." Lust never gets beyond gobbling grapes.

Gluttony

Gluttony today may be recognized by eating disorders and alcoholism. The lie—the good that is promised—is much the same as that of lust: pursuit of this practice will deaden psychic pain, and/or fill the soul's desperate hunger and emptiness. In moderation, there is nothing wrong with sometimes using food and drink as a reward—it may be practicing for the heavenly banquet. Perhaps the greatest help available today to get straight about how to be free of the immoderate and sinful use of food and drink is the twelve-step programs. They help people face their existential loneliness and be authentic. The truth is that nothing we ingest can fill the soul's hunger. Maybe that's what Jesus meant when he said, "I am the living water; I am the vine; I am the true bread."

Sloth

Sloth sounds like an old-fashioned sin, though in fact we may find it to be another besetting sin of our own times. In the Middle Ages it was called *acedia*, spiritual torpor. It is a peculiar quality of the sin of sloth, that persons or societies beset by it are both lethargic *and* restless. On the one hand they cannot find the energy to do anything worthwhile; on the other, they cannot truly be still and focused. They wander around aimlessly. In modern terms this sounds very much like what we might call a work disorder. Often workaholics who run themselves ragged all week striving after impossible achievements become evening and weekend couch potatoes. Whatever a person's work is, it is possible to feel desperately bored and over-burdened. There is not enough work to do; there is too much work to do. Both components of this attitude point to the lie that work will give meaning to our lives. It won't. It is our lives that give meaning to our work.

Sloth, which often resembles laziness, may not be so far from burnout—it may be the flip side of the coin. Burnout means there are no resources left, that a kind of functional bankruptcy is declared. The expectations that achievement will confer self-worth and that collapsing into stupor will bring heart's ease are both aspects of the same lie. The ancients fantasized a drug called nepenthe, which brought oblivion from all life's hardships and sorrows. Today, perhaps the drugs of choice serve the same craving as nepenthe might have once for oblivion or lowering of consciousness.

But the cost of sloth, either through mind-dulling activities or chemical substances, is too high. It doesn't bring peace. The hard way to true peace is a balanced discipline and a commitment to responsible awareness.

Anger

Anger isn't the preferred word for the sin because anger is a normal human feeling. It may be a divine "feeling" as well—in scripture we hear a good deal about the wrath of God. Anger is a signal that one's territory is being invaded. It may be our physical, psychological, or spiritual territory. An often-cited example of anger that is consonant with love is Jesus' overturning the tables of the moneychangers in the Temple. His, and God's, territory was being invaded. As we grow in life experience and love, we are more able to choose when and how to express our anger effectively. If we express anger, for instance, whenever someone takes the cookie we had our eyes on, people will not pay attention to our signal when a major violation occurs. It is a sort of "Wolf! Wolf!" situation.

For the manifestation of anger that is sin, we would prefer to use the word "hostility." Hostility takes over when anger shifts into the desire to put down or harm the other. The extreme manifestations of this choice against the good are aggression and violence. One false promise underlying the temptation is that acts of hostility will confer control, power, and the certainty of "might is right." But might is not necessarily right. Even if it were, it is not enough to be right. It is more important to be loving than to be right. Hostility often stockpiles rectitude and facts in its arsenal, but true power is the power of love which, contrary to putting down and destroying, builds up and creates.

THE SEVEN DEADLY SINS

The behavior, the false promise, and the truth
about how to get what we need.

Name	Behavior	The False Promise	The Truth
Pride	Narcissism Ego Inflation	Self-Esteem Perfection	Self-Knowledge Humility
Avarice	Accumulation Exploitation	Security Ease	Trust Gift
Envy	Wanting what one cannot have Judgmentalism	Self-Pity Justification	Self-Acceptance Respect of self and others
Lust	Sexual Addiction Fragmentation of sexuality	Fill soul's hunger to be loved	Commitment Intimacy
Gluttony	Addictions Eating Disorders Alcoholism	Affirmation Reward Fill the soul's hunger	Acknowledge bodily sustenance is not spiritual sustenance
Sloth	Irresponsibility Moral Bankruptcy Drop-out, burnout	Nepenthe or stupor masking as peace	Healthy discipline Responsibility Order
Anger	Violence Passive-aggression	Power, Control Certainty	Surrender Emptiness

What Sin Is, What It Is Not

It's necessary to say a bit more about what sin is and what it isn't. A word, then, about what sin is *not*. If we do not know that something is a sin, then for us it is not a sin. Here is a very mild example. Your room-mate (or spouse or child) comes home one evening and cries, "What a terrible day!" In response you say, "You've had a terrible day? Wait till you hear about *my* day . . ." Before you finish getting the words out, you see the hurt expression on the person's face and realize that if you continue on talking about *you* instead of that person, you will be choosing against the good—sinning. Up until that moment you weren't aware that such selfish nonattention to another is sinful, but after that you know it could be for *you*. If you choose to override that awareness with your own selfish agenda, that might be sin.

Sin is not mistakes. Sometimes we go into agonies over stupid mistakes we make. Mistakes are things like *honestly* thinking an appointment was for the same day next week (unlike the cover-ups fantasized about on the 79th Street cross-town bus discussed in chapter 3). Sometimes we feel more ashamed about some mistakes we make than we do about our actual sins.

Sin is also not temptation. Some of the classic writers in Western spirituality have noted gradations in what is and what is not sin, which people today may think nitpicky to the point of laughter.

First, thoughts that spring to one's mind are not sin, they are just thoughts. Second, and most important, when some thoughts become temptations, they are just temptations. Temptation is not sin. Every human being is tempted. Jesus, being completely human, was "tested as we are" (Hebrews 4:15). Jesus teaches us to pray that we will not be led into temptation, because we *can* choose the lesser good, the evil. Resisting temptation is no fun, and we are wise to pray to be spared that test.

So how does an unsinful thought become sinful? The spiritual writers identify a next stage called "delectation" from Latin *"delectatio,"* to delight. What this means is that when a thought becomes a temptation, we welcome it and start enjoying it, tasting it as if it were a hard candy we were rolling around on our tongue. Delectation also is not yet sin. However, this stage is dangerous to fool around with. If we entertain such thoughts (or as someone is reported to have said: "I don't entertain them, they entertain me!"), then we are liable to enter the next stage that is called "consent," which *is* sin. This is the point at which we might say to ourselves: "As soon as I get a chance I will do it." Just as it is not always easy for us to distinguish how conscious a choice to sin is, so it is also not always easy to know the exact point at which delectation becomes consent. Only God knows for sure.

Now, having taken a look at the range of what goes on in our minds from unbidden thoughts all the way to actual consent to sin, let's take a look at what outright sin has to do with accepting the complete, authentic human. Take the story of David in the Bible. David was "a man after [God's] heart" (Acts 13:22). Why? David was an adulterer and a murderer among other sinful things; his actions reeked of greed, lust, envy, and violence. And he, too, like the rest of us, was tempted to deny and avoid conscious knowledge of this. He was lucky enough, however, to be confronted by the prophet Nathan (2 Samuel 12). The thing is, when David was faced with the ugly truth about himself, he accepted it, repented, and got straight with God. It was not David's good works or sinless life that made him a man after God's own heart. It was his courageous honesty in acknowledging his own sin and repenting of it.

The Problem with Being Judgmental

People are, in general, too self-judgmental. And this is a problem for a number of reasons. The sources of self-judging go back to what we were discussing in the chapter on the myth of perfection. People measure themselves against ideals they have learned from family, peers, and the general culture, and inevitably find themselves wanting. They judge themselves against these unrealistic norms.

The problem manifests itself in various guises. Self-judgment, for example, takes the form of extreme anxiety—exhibiting classical symptoms of anxiety neurosis and panic attacks. Others' judgment of their own shortcomings is a root cause of depression. And then there are the people who try to ease the pain of their self-judgment by blaming other people and external causes for their unhappiness. Some of us succumb to the temptation of putting down others in order to make ourselves look better and feel better. All of these manifestations of self-judgment are dangerous. They can be externalized in a range of behaviors from small, daily acts of abuse and unkindness, to extreme rage and, yes, may even lead to murder and holocaust. If we can only begin to accept ourselves, we can move to a healthy self-compassion, and only then to being truly understanding of and compassionate to others.

Moving toward Self-Forgiveness

Some people grow up accepting themselves, but for most of us, self-acceptance isn't easy. Usually before self-acceptance, there has to be self-forgiveness. The more decades of self-judgment that people inflict on themselves, the harder self-forgiveness can become.

One of the ways of thinking about forgiveness, especially in some Christian circles, is that we should forgive immediately, sight unseen. Not being able to do this has itself been for many a major cause of self-condemnation.

Think of the practice of the governor's pardon. Before a governor can grant a pardon to a sentenced criminal, there must be a prescribed series of events. First, there has to be a collection of evidence, then there has to be a trial, then a verdict, *and the verdict must be "guilty."* Finally, a sentence follows. Then, and only then, can a pardon be granted. Many Christians have a terrible time getting the sequence straight. They try to collect evidence, have a trial, and grant the pardon all at the same time, or in reverse order: they try to grant pardon before the guilty verdict is pronounced!

Granted that the practice of law does not take into account the free grace of the Spirit—yet the analogy may be useful. In order to forgive, there must be clarity on what there is to forgive. It helps if the offending party asks for forgiveness, but if that is not to be, forgiveness is still possible if the evidence has been clearly ascertained, the trial well conducted, and the verdict decisive.

Seven Lively Steps to Forgiveness

Now, about ways we can move to self-forgiveness. Like forgiving our parents or anybody else, self-forgiveness cannot be an instantaneous thing. It may be a lengthy and painful process. In a fanciful balance to the "Seven Deadly Sins," we called these "The Seven Lively Steps to Forgiveness."

1. The first step is the realization that we are lovable and loved. For many who have had painful and confusing childhood experiences of love, it is very difficult to trust the constant, nourishing love of God or of any human being. We must be able to open ourselves to, and if we can, pray for the ability to know ourselves capable of receiving unconditional love, that is, love no matter what we have done.

2. The second step, even if we have made only a bare beginning at this, is to face up to the evil we recognize in ourselves—that which *is* unlovable, unacceptable. This will include those things that stem from our neg-

ative programming—that may have come from all the myths we have been filled up with *and* our willful choices against the good as we have known it. It will take all the discerning we have learned to sort this out as best we can.

3. The third step is to make the choice to accept (not condone, but acknowledge) the evil as part of our whole perception of ourselves, rather than to deny or try to exterminate it.

4. As a fourth step, we must realize that the milieu of this work is called truth. That where we go to enter this clearest dimension of our understanding is our own deepest reality.

5. The fifth step is to recognize that God is Truth, and that God meets us precisely in this milieu of our own truth—not where we think we should be, or would like to be, or feel others need us to be, but where we *are*. God is Truth, that which is. When Moses, standing before the burning bush, demanded to know whom to say sent him, God said, "Tell them 'I Am' sent you." We are made in God's image—we are that which we are. We are not "I should be," but "I am."

6. The sixth step is to know, therefore, that the acceptance of one's own evil must become a part of one's truth, of one's relationship with God. A scriptural example of this is the story of David in the Old Testament.

7. The seventh step is perhaps especially difficult for those of us who have lived long decades with self-blame, guilt, and shame. As we have bravely faced the evil in ourselves, we must now, with equal integrity, acknowledge the good—the gifts and graces we have been given—by our nature, our nurture, and by God. And not least, those good gifts and aspects of ourselves for which we can take at least part credit because of our choosing what good we were able. As we try to empty ourselves of a focus on the evil in ourselves to concentrate on what real *good* we can

find, we help prepare the soil for the seeds of self-compassion and reconciliation. After some practice this should feel like a shift from guilt to
gratitude. The process may include some tears, first of compunction and
repentance, then of relief and even joy.

As stated earlier, this may be a lengthy and painful process; we make a
start by believing that it's possible—this procedure of coming to a stance
of compassion and joy toward ourselves, God, and others. Analytic psychotherapy is a great help for many people in identifying false guilt and
negative programming and in facilitating the movement to greater self-
knowledge and acceptance. Carl Rogers said that therapy is the process of
assimilating denied experience. Also, as in the case of King David,
prophetic, that is, God-inspired spiritual guidance can often facilitate
much of the same work.

A final question may arise about all the negative matter we unearth in
the process of awareness—and especially our sins. What do we do with it?
The classical answer is, "Give it to God." This may seem a strange, if not
disturbing answer. Here's a story to illustrate it. From all accounts Saint
Jerome was not an easy person to get along with—an irascible, opinion-
ated, though intensely dedicated man. One Advent, or pre-Christmas
season, he decided to go into the wilderness for a retreat. As he said his
prayers, it came to him to make some spiritual "birthday gift" to the
Christ Child. The saint prayed and thought and then addressed God: "I
will dedicate to you the fruit of my scholarship—my translation of the
scriptures into the common tongue, the Vulgate." But there seemed to be
a strange silence in the heavenly places as if, in fact, his gift had not been
accepted. So he thought and prayed a while longer. Then he said to God:
"I understand, you don't want my great scholarship—you are more interested in my discipline and austerity of life. I dedicate that to you!" But
again the heavenly silence. Back to his prayers. Then, "Aha!" he

exclaimed. "You don't want my austerities, you want my devotions—the fervent love of my heart!" Incredibly, the heavens were still silent. Jerome was feeling peeved and at the point of giving up the whole idea. "Then what?" he cried to God in total frustration. "What can I give to you?" Clear as clear in his mind the answer came: "Give me your sins, my son. Those are the only things I have not first given you." Why would God want our sins? Because sin and suffering are the raw material of glory. God can take all of reality and fashion it into glory—even to the horror and humiliation of the crucifixion.

As the seed must be broken open in order to sprout, as every baby is born out of pain, so creation groans and travails (Romans 8:22) to bring the world into the kingdom. The sins as well as the creativity of humanity are part of the stuff of reality that is in the process of transfiguration. Because we are made in the image of God, we are called in love to be co-creators in this metamorphosis. We can choose to participate, each one according to the grace we have been given. We are called to emptying and integration, individually and in community. We are called into "maturity, to the measure of the full stature of Christ" (Ephesians 4:13). And the way to do this is the process of forgiveness and reconciliation. The point of forgiveness, its heart and its end, is new life.

SECTION 2

Filling Up with the Spirit

CHAPTER EIGHT

Transition

Myth: The best way to make it through any transition is to hold on to that with which one is familiar in order to avoid falling apart.

Truth: Transition is about letting go or emptying oneself of attachments to the known in order to make room for something new.

W e have been describing cultural myths that create barriers to moving toward spiritual freedom and wholeness. The purpose of describing the myths in such detail is to become more aware of the forces that influence us in our daily lives. But it is not enough just to become aware of these forces. At any given moment, we have the option of emptying ourselves of cultural myths and going for something that more closely resembles our deepest desires and passions. Such a change isn't done all at once; it requires transition. As we empty ourselves of the oppressive cultural lies and myths, it is natural to ask: now what? We are on a threshold, in a process of change, in a time of transition. The vessel is empty—where is the replacement?

Transition brings challenges as we move from being filled with cultural myths and the agendas of others to moving toward embracing that which is unique to each one of us. To settle for anything less than embracing our deepest desires in communion with others is to ignore the truth or the will of God.

Many of us learn through socialization that the way you get along in life is to go along. This is one of the reasons we have had a section in each chapter on the three main sources of such influence: family systems, peer groups, and culture. If we know these sources of influence, we can spend less time blindly adopting what others think and spend more time listening to our own sense of what is right for us. We can be one who honors both what others say and what the still, small voice within is saying. We can listen to our own deepest yearnings—working hard to hear them over the din of the cultural noise we internalize. We are ready for the transition.

A typical part of the process of transition is that we go along accepting many of the beliefs others impose upon us, doing what we are told, until a shocking event intervenes and dismantles our defense system. C. S. Lewis

Doug: A Story of Transition

Doug's transition began with the discovery at the age of 28 that he had been adopted at birth. This realization was the catalytic event that gave him permission to question all of the cultural myths he had become filled with over almost three decades of life. As Doug tells the story:

"The hardest part of the transition was figuring out how to empty myself of the myths that were clearly no longer working, without my life completely falling apart. As part of the search for answers, I attended a community-building workshop in 1993 led by ES and others that helped participants through the transition from fullness to emptiness to becoming filled with the spirit. In that workshop, a safe environment was created that allowed individuals to surface and empty out enormously painful experiences that had happened to them. I told my adoption story that weekend and was amazed to find that I could reveal what I thought was a horrible secret about myself and not be condemned for it.

"As transformational as that first workshop was, it was not sufficient to get me through this transition. ES agreed to meet with me periodically for some time after that, and her spiritual guidance has been critical to my being able to navigate the unknown terrain of emptiness and the spirit without becoming lost. While the process of transition can be navigated alone, it is much easier to manage within the context of a supportive community and/or with the help of a guide."

referred to this as nothing less than a wake-up call from God. We may not be doing what we are called to do but rather what everyone else is calling us to do. And because different people have different agendas for us, we spend a lot of time going in different directions.

We said earlier in the book that God may respond to our question of what to do by saying "Here is a blank canvas, paint me a picture." The artist is doing the work of God by projecting images from the deepest part of his or her psyche onto canvas. Even those of us who can't paint are called to do the same thing with our lives, but the noise of cultural beliefs and others' opinions block such authentic creativity. Transition is about unblocking the pathways to those deepest parts of who we are.

Many theologians and philosophers have described the transition as going from being broken to becoming whole or from having fallen to being redeemed. For many, the problem is being too full. We are full of what other people think, and the transition is about moving from a state of fullness to emptiness; emptying out the images and beliefs of others to discover our own deepest desires.

As we reach the point of transition, we may hear our inner dialogue: I have worked very hard to get to this point in my life. And sure, the persona I have created is really just an amalgamation of other people's beliefs, but it's taken my whole lifetime to build it. Am I going to throw it all away just because it's a little unpleasant? My life isn't a sell-out to the forces of darkness . . . is it? And another thing. I don't see anyone else in my world looking for the narrow road toward spiritual enlightenment. Everyone else seems to be content with working forty or more hours a week, fighting rush-hour traffic, and going home to a hurried dinner, hassles with the kids, vegetative time in front of the television, and then going to bed. Are these people all following their deepest desire? Or are they so filled with the rules and beliefs of others that their own yearnings have long since been drowned out?

Writers throughout the ages have described this in a variety of ways, but the pattern is roughly the same. We are born as divine creations of God, each given a unique identity and set of gifts. Then we move into the world and begin to fill ourselves up with the beliefs and "things" of the existential world and our unique gifts fade into the distance. At some point, we begin to feel hollow and restless and ask: Is this all there is? Often around midlife a catalyzing event (loss of job, divorce, health crisis, death of a loved one) cracks open the shell of armor we have built around ourselves and for the first time we begin to question our life. This becomes the most important moment in a person's life. The MacArthur Foundation's study on midlife calls these moments "psychological turning points."

When we reach this critical turning point, we can chose to convert (which literally means to turn around) to a new way of living or we can try to just shake it off and decide that nothing has really changed (but thank God the crisis is over) and go back to living the way we had been living before. The person who chooses to change or make the transition from the old way of living to a new way is beginning to empty the vessel.

Finding a Guide for the Transition

It is critically important for anyone seeking to make this kind of transition to find a guide or a small group of people with whom to work in this process.

It is a tremendously freeing idea to choose one's own mentors. One of our colleagues once described how she has her own personal board of directors: twelve people who have agreed to serve as her advisors, just like a board directs the affairs of an organization. They don't necessarily meet as a group but rather are available as consultants or confidants. You may not choose to formally ask people to serve in this function officially, but you might instead have a list of folks you consider to be on your personal board of directors. It should be an interesting mix of wise people and friends. Who would you choose for such an assignment?

Because we learn from one another, it is very important to find at least one person, if not a group or tribe, to understand and encourage us as we go through the transition.

To a great extent it seems to be true that "When the student is ready, the teacher will appear." Most often the teacher is a person who has accomplished his or her own transition and has been living the "examined life." But sometimes the first intimation of being understood and encouraged can be found in a book or even in a piece of music. As one grows in the awareness, one may find more and more people who are of "the tribe," who have a talent for reality.

When a person has *not* found an understanding supporter and feels alone in the dark, it can be tragic. One of the most poignant scenes in Shakespeare is when Hamlet's school friends, Rosencrantz and Gildenstern, betray him. They choose to join Hamlet's mother and step-father in the lies and cover-up around the murder of Hamlet's father. Ophelia is too young and emotionally fragile to understand and support. Polonius, whose age should be accompanied by wisdom, is no help. In his schoolmate, Horatio, Hamlet has a man whose friendship is solid as a rock, but it is not clear how understanding Horatio is of what his friend is going through. Horatio is a support, but not a mentor.

One of the most telling scenes in the film *Amadeus* is Salieri's admission to being the patron saint of the mediocre. We feel Mozart's pain at having no "tribe," no one person to understand his genius.

We, too, might feel that there is no one there with us in the dark. In that time of seeming dereliction, divine compassion himself—Jesus—will come to us as the one who understands and supports.

It must be said that no other human being or tribe of human beings can fully alleviate existential loneliness. As Saint Augustine wrote: "O Lord, You have made us for yourself, and our hearts shall find no rest until they find their rest in You." However, the paradox is that we are called to encourage and support one another, in cooperation with grace, as we seek the truth of our humanity.

Along with the spiritual guide, it helps in searching for your own deepest desires (God's will as opposed to the will of others) to study the wisdom literature—the most common examples being in the Bible: Job, Psalms, Proverbs, Ecclesiastes, and Song of Solomon. When one looks at the literature, it is filled with descriptions that help one continue. A key message of the Hebrew scriptures is about the importance of emptiness: in effect, God is saying that when you were in the desert and had nothing, you believed. Once you arrived into civilization and gained comfort, your faith weakened.

The Process of Emptying

While transition is about beginning to question the rules and obligations of society, the myths we have been discussing thus far, there are many more rules and obligations, values, and beliefs that we have internalized that are someone else's arbitrary view of reality. They must be examined. The image of the child here is a familiar one. Jesus evoked the image to describe the kingdom: "In order to enter the kingdom of heaven, one must become like a child." What is meant here is that one must go back to the time when we were empty of all the things that caused us to forget our divine origins. Wordsworth says in "Intimations of Immortality": "From God, who is our home / Heaven lies about us in our infancy!"

The goal of the transition is to return to that sense of original inno-cence when we were filled with the spirit of boundless potential and energy, born from our proximity to the Divine Creator.

We can curse the process and resist it or we can accept it and say, "If so, then what?" Once we see that it is about loading up and then empty-ing out cultural myths and lies and involves the full range of human emo-tions, how are we to cope? Recognizing that the process is filled with both joy and pain, good and bad, makes it much easier to cope with the inevitable bumps along the way: the disapproving family members, the questioning neighbors, the judgment-filled coworkers.

All of the things that happen are part of the process of moving toward spiritual freedom and are necessary. The pain of transition is easier when we understand that it is an essential part of emptying the vessel and fill-ing it with spiritual maturity. We must trust the spirit, the deepest desires within us. What is propelling us is our authentic self.

God calls us to authenticity, to honor our own thoughts and emotions and beliefs, not to be possessed by those of others. This is God's deepest wish for us. To this end, the freedom comes in having a single source of direction rather than a hundred conflicting ones. It comes from the absolute belief that each individual is put on this earth for a purpose that is different from all others. It comes from the knowledge that those deep-est beliefs really *are* God's will. Finally, freedom comes from the evidence you will begin to see that trust and faith from within will never steer you wrong. There may be bumps along the road, but each is an inevitable part of moving toward wholeness.

Once we make the transition to the spiritual path, the realization comes that everything that happens, good and bad, joyful and painful, beautiful and ugly, *all of it*, is exactly what is needed for us to become com-plete human beings.

A diagram integrates a number of the concepts we have been describing. This diagram represents the cycle of the typical human life: beginning with "The True Self" and then moving toward the stage of the seven myths we have been discussing: perfection, control, accumulation, limitlessness, individualism, happiness, and the myth of being good. We create the "social self" that is burdened with not only the cultural lies but also the effects of having internalized them: stress, isolation, judgment.

TOWARD SPIRITUAL FREEDOM

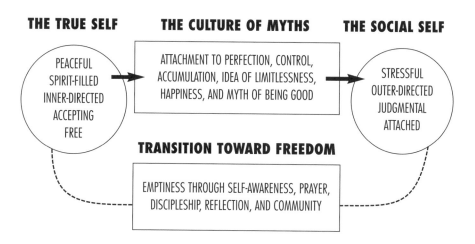

THE TRUE SELF   **THE CULTURE OF MYTHS**   **THE SOCIAL SELF**

PEACEFUL SPIRIT-FILLED INNER-DIRECTED ACCEPTING FREE

ATTACHMENT TO PERFECTION, CONTROL, ACCUMULATION, IDEA OF LIMITLESSNESS, HAPPINESS, AND MYTH OF BEING GOOD

STRESSFUL OUTER-DIRECTED JUDGMENTAL ATTACHED

TRANSITION TOWARD FREEDOM

EMPTINESS THROUGH SELF-AWARENESS, PRAYER, DISCIPLESHIP, REFLECTION, AND COMMUNITY

The key to moving toward spiritual freedom is emptying oneself of those beliefs that are getting in the way of authentically connecting with oneself, with others, and with God. The process of self-emptying is an unavoidable stage for those wishing to move beyond the social self. It should be entered into with excitement and enthusiasm rather than with dread and fear. For the goal is to reach the stage of the child or the True Self: a self free from addiction, open to new experience, connected to the source of creation, filled with the spirit of peace, and accepting of oneself and others.

You might start by asking, "Where am I?" Am I still in that blissful stage of innocence where I feel free to be my true self or am I in the process of becoming burdened, accepting the opinions and rules of others in order to go along. Am I beginning to realize that such a burden is no longer working, and I feel like I am wandering in search of meaning?

Too many of us have not figured out how to make the turn, if you will, and begin the process of emptying what has filled our vessel over our lifetime. Our hope is that by gaining a clearer picture of the end, the payoff, which is to be a vessel of peace and freedom, more of us will begin to take the risk. You may be saying, "So I go through all of this filling up with the rules of society, then turn and spend the rest of my life emptying all the beliefs and rules that have burdened me, only to end up exactly where I started? Is this some kind of cruel divine joke?"

It is no joke, but far be it for us to speculate why it is this way. All we can do is learn as much as we can and try to engage in life with a calmness at the center that never wavers. The Zen way of experiencing reality fully but then letting it go may be a key to surviving the tough spots of this transition.

Employing a kind of detached engagement can lead to a profound and divine transformation if we are willing to be patient and experience the pain, joy, and ambiguity that arise along the way. It's the second innocence, or the simplicity on the other side of complexity. And while we may arrive in the same place, it will not look the same.

The Necessity for Transition

Aristotle said that man by nature is a political animal. Political, as used here, refers back to its Greek root in *polis*, a city, indicating that human beings naturally live in community. Saint Paul used the analogy of being individual members of one body. We are social and interactive creatures by nature; no one can exist in a totally detached way. The only way that human beings learn how to be human beings is from each other. So, yes, we do have to go through the emptying of cultural dictates since we fill up with not only genetic tendencies but also some form of cultural, tribal, and family myth.

One thing that is always passed down is the concept of *"ought."* C. S. Lewis wrote in *Mere Christianity,* "Human beings, all over the earth, have this curious idea that they ought to behave in a certain way, and cannot really get rid of it. Secondly, that they do not in fact behave in that way."

This human capacity for choosing right and wrong, and knowing we often choose "wrong," is passed down generation after generation and may be thought of as "original sin." Along with the sense of sin, we inherit guilt. And we take on a load of ways to repress or minimize our wrong choices and subsequent guilt.

Cultural lies offer ways to ignore our fallibility and to avoid making hard choices for the good. They are lies partly because they claim that perfection, control, limitlessness, goodness, and so forth are—or should be—easily attainable and that we can escape from guilt and powerlessness. Our myths advertise a wide gate and an easy road. But, as we have said before, the reality of spiritual formation is not easy—"The gate is narrow and the road is hard that leads to life" (Matthew 7:14).

Some people do find and choose the road to life. The good news is that, along with the lies that are loaded on us, the call to break out of them is also passed down. If there is original sin, there is, as Matthew Fox has written in a book of the same name, original blessing. There is a universal invitation to liberation and to holiness. From the fairy tales of The Ugly

Duckling and The Emperor's New Clothes, to *Hamlet* and *King Lear*, literature is full of tales of the struggle to break out of the bondage of cultural expectations and find freedom in the truth no matter what the cost. Most often, the truth-speaker is either a child, a madman or, as in the case of *King Lear*, a Fool.

Challenges of the Transition

Three "challenging things" come to mind about the transition through emptiness to truth: fear of the unknown, fear of vulnerability, and fear of commitment.

First, a word about the **fear of the unknown**. In classical spiritual literature there is a stage that Saint John of the Cross called "The Dark Night of the Senses." It is a stage where things of the senses—food, drink, gold, toys of all sorts—no longer satisfy the way they once did. The question arises: "Is this all there is?" Another way of viewing it is that the lowest two stages on the model of the Four Levels of Human Happiness (page 42), physical pleasure and ego satisfaction, no longer seem enough for happiness. But the soul has not yet become proficient in living according to spiritual values. It's like being in the state where a tadpole is turning into a frog. The little amphibian is losing its gills and having to breathe a rarefied atmosphere with brand new tiny lungs; it is losing the long tail that was so handy for swimming, and it is not yet proficient on these clumsy new legs for land use. Being in between, being in the dark, is scary and disorienting. (Disorienting is the exact word—literally it means not knowing which way is east.)

In the same way, we ask, What am I? Am I nothing? Living in the unknown is new and fearful. As is so often the case, Shakespeare puts his finger on the temptation to give up the struggle: "Makes us rather bear those ills we have / Than fly to others that we know not of."

The second challenge follows closely: the **fear of vulnerability** or, literally, of being *wound-able*. People who are in the transition to truth or who have made the transition are often identified as prime targets for popular censure. The wounds can range from ridicule—accusations of being weird—to actual damage, such as being fired from one's job or imprisoned for one's beliefs. In its most extreme form, breaking out of the cultural lies can be fatal—witness Socrates being compelled to drink hemlock, or Jesus' crucifixion, or Martin Luther King Jr.'s assassination.

A curious dynamic asserts itself here. There is something in human nature that tends to exalt spiritual heroes before it brings them low. "The bigger they are, the harder they fall" mentality delights in setting up the truth-sayers before cutting them down. There are Palm Sunday hosannas before Good Friday savagery.

Of course, innumerable people make the transition to spiritual truth and freedom without suffering major hostility from others. Mother Teresa of Calcutta is one case in point, though even she had to leave one community to start another. But a fear of what the cost *might* be is realistic. An adventure into the unknown is always scary. The good news, though, is that there is help. An assurance of this is in Deuteronomy (33:27 KJV): "The eternal God is thy refuge, and underneath are the everlasting arms."

Finally, for some souls in transition there is the **fear of commitment**. There may be anxiety that if one responds to the call to the way of truth, more will be demanded than one is able to give. We get cold feet because we fear that the cost will be more than we are able to pay. The great cry at this point is, "Why me? Why can't I just stay a safe little me?"

ES: The Story of Transition

When ES was about thirty, a friend was going on a retreat to a convent and convinced ES to accompany her. ES tells the story:

"It was the first time for both of us and we were a little scared. Once at the convent, the silence was powerful. I walked out onto the grounds and into the little wood that bordered the property; the foliage was brilliant with color and sunlight in the autumn day. I began to feel an inner pressure, an invitation, to commit myself to something; gradually this something defined itself as the 'inner way,' the way of truth-seeking, no matter what the cost.

"This was frightening—I couldn't know what the cost might involve. It was a crisis of trust. I deliberately put my commitment on hold, and thought and tried to pray about other things for the remainder of my walk. When it was almost time for the community to say Vespers—evening prayers—I went into the chapel. I knelt down and the 'invitation' came back with more force and a sort of gentle urgency. It seemed that the high walls were lined with invisible presences, as if the very air were alive and waiting for my response. 'Give me a little more time,' I said. 'The Sisters will be coming in any minute now for Vespers—I need more time.'

"After the prayer service the Sisters and other guests all filed out, and I was left there alone. After a time of holding off—of preparation, I suppose—I breathed deeply and said silently into the expectancy: 'Yes! Yes! I will, I will go for the truth no matter what the cost. All right—YES!' And it was as if that assent and commitment were received, that they would now and henceforth be kept and honored in whatever space or dimension such promises are held.

"The experience made very real to me both the profundity of the challenge, and the blessing of the invitation to venture into the mystery of reality."

The Paradox of Emptying While Becoming Full

In the first chapter we talked about how human beings develop or ripen from the natural narcissism of infancy to the mature capacity for self-gift. There is a parallel in spiritual development. We mature into the capacity to serve others. It is most often true that at the beginning of the spiritual search, after one has made the commitment to divine reality, there is a certain self-centeredness. This, like the other infancy, is not reproachable, but rather a natural stage in growth. When we are newborn in life, love, or spirit, there is a period of self-absorption. In human love it is an absorption with each other; in divine love it is an absorption with God for one's own sake. Since God orders this ripening process, it is not surprising that it is in this beginning stage, this "honeymoon period," that spiritual gifts and consolations are showered on the soul like gifts from a lover.

Saint Bernard, a monk of the twelfth century, wrote a treatise, *On Loving God.* In it he describes four degrees of human love for God. First we love ourselves for our own sake; then we love God for our own sake; third we love God for God's sake; and finally we love ourselves for God's sake. It is at this last, most mature stage that we have enough self-love in God to be filled and overflow. A corollary to "You can't give what you don't have" is perhaps "When you abound you are impelled to give." When a mother's breasts are full of milk for her child, it is painful **not** to give it.

Yes, love must act. Love is generative—it yearns to extend and perpetuate itself. If water does not run, if it is not "living water," it becomes stagnant. It is great good news that just as we human beings pass down cultural lies and the potential to choose against love, so also there is positive programming—the passing down of loving encouragement. This may be accomplished by good parenting and/or caring guidance. The reclamation of discipleship would go a long way toward alleviating the isolation of individualism.

So, the question becomes, can we become fully empty of the negative to return to the divine innocence—can we become fully empty in order to become full? This is essentially the question Nicodemus asked Jesus. "How can anyone be born after having grown old? Can one enter a second time into the mother's womb and be born?" Jesus' answer, as reported in the Gospel of John, is a bit oblique, but essentially he says, "Yes, indeed" (John 3:4).

We have mentioned the two simplicities—one on this side and one on the other side of complexity; there are correspondingly two kinds of innocence. Perhaps it is not too fanciful to say that the first lies on this side of the law of the knowledge of good and evil. The second lies on the other side. It has nothing to do with ignorance, but rather with a wisdom in spirit that transcends the letter of the law.

There may be a relationship between this second innocence and what we have called emptiness. Both are represented as a kind of third stage. Both the first innocence and what in community-building is called *pseudo-community* have aspects in common. Both have very little knowledge of differences and conflict and little experience of suffering. If children have considerable conflict and suffering, we tend to say they have been robbed of their innocence. The first innocence, sooner or later, like the first simplicity, moves into complexity and the knowledge of good and evil.

There is a way to move beyond complexity and the reliance upon knowledge, which entails the acceptance of paradox and finally of mystery; we can never figure it all out. The new physicists have come to a kind of Socratic declaration: "I only know that I do not know." Both complexity and chaos are stages of growth out of first-stage simplicities. They are transitional stages. They in turn may be transcended by an emptiness and second simplicity that make space to receive the spirit of divine reality and new life. This freedom and ripening is always in process. It is not somewhere to get to or be complacent in.

We probably won't meet the person who would say, "Now I am totally empty," or "Now I am divinely innocent." The point of being empty is to invite the spirit of community; the point of being innocent is to invite the spirit of holy wisdom. The closest declaration is most likely Saint Paul's saying: "It is no longer I who live, but it is Christ who lives in me" (Galatians 2:20). Even there it is obvious that Paul's personality is still very much in process. Paul has become simplified and emptied to the extent that Christ's spirit of love and truth are able to be held and perceived, though still "in a glass, darkly."

As long as we have freedom to choose, we are free to go in and out of or deeper into this innocence. There is a certain sense in which one does not go back again into the *same* complexity or the *same* chaos. There is a sense that one is no longer "going" anywhere. But neither is the mystery of inner wisdom or divine innocence a static thing. Anyone can regress or relapse. Everyone can go deeper into oneness.

The quality of divine innocence is not romantic but rather it is real in the most profound sense. It recognizes and assimilates memory of past experience and vision of future potential, to focus them simply in the now-moment. It knows that the present is held in eternity, which is glory. This second innocence discerns the difference between license and the true liberty of the children of God. The peace of this second innocence is beyond understanding. Its joy is radiant with the spontaneity of love. It is the pearl of great price, which is worth any cost.

C H A P T E R   N I N E

Filling Up with the Spirit

Truth: The transition from seeking acceptance by conform-
ing to cultural myth, through a time of emptiness, to
becoming a vessel of peace is not to be underestimated in
difficulty. It is important to emphasize that the point of
emptying oneself of cultural myths is not to reject the world
around us and retreat to some secluded cabin in the woods.
Rather, the point is to become free to more fully connect
with the world by making room for and inviting God.

Many people in this age of reason and science are generally skeptical of anything that cannot be proven scientifically. That skepticism easily turns to cynicism when we hear story after story of public figures who experience a religious conversion or profound humility only after getting caught in a crime or peccadillo. Or, we are skeptical of anything that does not generate profit. Bill Gates, when asked by a reporter if he attended church, said he had never found it to be time-efficient. That seems to summarize the view for many of us who are racing as fast as we can down the information superhighway and simply don't see the payoff to attending church or spending time in prayer.

To make matters worse, the Western culture of individualism has made it problematic to rely on God. God is too often viewed as some indefinable, silent force, popular primarily among those who are either naïve or who have messed up and are looking for a way out.

Nevertheless, we do find ourselves in the midst of a major resurgence of interest in the spiritual and holy, both among the young and the aging baby boomers confronting their own mortality. We are asking the questions and desiring to be filled with what is true rather than the lies and myths to which we have been subjected.

As we empty the vessel of the old wine, making ready for the new, there are two important transition points: church and prayer. Both have often presented themselves as barriers. However, during the infilling of the new, it's important to rid church and prayer of cultural myths and lies, too, so we can appropriate them in the way God intends.

What about Church?

Mainstream religious institutions have historically been the primary source of answers to our spiritual questions. Interestingly, the two fastest-growing kinds of institutions are on polar extremes in terms of their philosophies. On one end, there are the ultra-conservative institutions that are narrowly proscriptive in their approach and attract people who want certainty in a rapidly changing society where there is a perception that morals and traditional values are in decline. Conservative churches provide certainty in an uncertain world and many of them are experiencing record growth rates.

On the other end of the continuum, there are the rapidly growing institutions that express themselves as ecumenical or interdenominational. They are congregations that honor the individual nature of each congregant and believe that the glory of God's creation lies in honoring the absolute uniqueness of each and every individual. These institutions minimize specific proscriptions about the way a truly godly person should act and emphasize that the point is to worship regularly, in whatever form that worship might take.

Despite the resurgence of interest in things spiritual, there is still a major disconnection between those interested in spirituality and the number of people attending church regularly. Surveys show that some 40 percent of Americans report attending church once per week, with 90 percent of all Americans saying they believe in a higher power. This is a wide discrepancy between worshiping corporately and believing. Part of the reason for many individuals' resistance to joining mainstream religious institutions is that so many people have been damaged by them. A common joke among psychiatrists is that if it weren't for religious institutions and the patients they generated, their practices would have gone under a long time ago.

Negative experiences with institutional religion aren't uncommon. A few people have been so severely damaged at a vulnerable age that they may never be healed of the evil they were subjected to in the name of

God. At the other end of the spectrum, some disenchanted people have the experience of church not being negative enough even to call "bad"— perhaps it was just "blah." And, of course, there are many people whose early church experience was at various places between the extremes of horrifying and tepid. Some of these folk call themselves "believers," perhaps more speak of themselves as "lapsed" or "former" believers.

People having problems with "church" can point to countless contemporary examples of the sins of religious institutions and the people in them manipulating the power bestowed. One clever 1992 film, *Leap of Faith*, gives the amusing fictional account of just such manipulation. Traveling faith-healer/evangelist Jonas Nightingale has a traveling healing "ministry." As the faithful walk into the ministry's tent, his "disciples" learn facts about them and then transmit those facts to another disciple, a computer whiz who logs the personal data into a computer program based on where the unsuspecting congregant is seated. The disciple then has a transmitter used to give these facts to Jonas on stage.

Jonas calls out the names of these people one by one and recites facts that "only a man of God" could have known about them. Later in the movie, Jonas discusses the upcoming performance with a disciple who worries that the local law enforcement people will catch them unless people are actually being healed. To which Jonas says "Remember our insurance policy: God can only heal you if your faith is strong enough." The implication is that if anyone questioned his faith-healing effectiveness, he would just say, "Well, I guess your faith isn't strong enough to be healed." Sound familiar?

So what are we to do with the skepticism and cynicism that real-life human manipulations of religion and faith have left us with? How do we get past the fact that many of the institutions of religion are run by human beings who themselves have flaws? Or, simply, why go to church?

There isn't a short, simple response. But, if we return to true meanings, we can find the answer.

The beginning of church for Christians is what happened on the Thursday night before the Friday Jesus was arrested and killed. We call it Maundy Thursday because *maunde* (from Latin *mandare*) was related to the Middle English for "commandment." Jesus didn't give a lot of commandments; mostly he told stories. But that Thursday night he did give us two commandments. He commanded us to love one another, and he also enjoined us to "Do this in remembrance of me." There is one basic reason for the institutional church and that is that Jesus instituted it when he said, "Do this."

Do what? Break bread and eat it, pour wine and drink it, all of us, in fellowship. So we do it. The friends and followers of Jesus have been doing this as the good news spread around the world ever since that last supper. Saying the prayers, breaking the bread, remembering Jesus, and telling the good news.

That Thursday night Jesus knew he was not going to be with his friends in the same familiar, human way much longer. He knew Judas was negotiating with the authorities who were out to get him and that his earthly life was coming to an end. He was aware of our human needs, and he well understood the truth behind the story we told in chapter 3 about the lonely child who wanted a God "with skin on." Jesus knew this was the way for him to be with us and strengthen us, to remain our Lord.

By the way, English-speaking people have a great blessing in the use of the word "Lord" for Jesus. The romance languages use derivations of the Latin *dominus*, from which we get words like "dominate." But "lord" comes from the Anglo-Saxon *hlafweard* which means "bread keeper" (from *hlaf* we get "loaf" and from *weard* we get words like "warden" and "guardian"). So in our language, Lord Jesus is not a figure of domination, but the keeper and giver of bread. And we are his companions. Switching to Latin, we note that "companion" comes from roots meaning "with" and "bread." We share with the one who called himself the "living bread that came down from heaven" and promised "the bread that I will give for the life of the world is my flesh" (John 6:51).

So why do we need church today? In a profound way, that gift and that sustaining power provide a centering force in our lives. We live in a culture of specialization; fragmentation is not too strong a word. We hear distressing phrases like "coming unglued" and "falling apart." It is no wonder that people in this culture often feel splintered and fragmented.

As humans, we are prone to polarize things like body and spirit, mind and matter, which cannot *actually* be separated. So we need a way to focus and center all the dimensions of our life experience. Philosopher Mircea Eliade wrote: "A universe comes to birth from its center; it spreads out from a central point that is, as it were, its navel . . . the Center is precisely . . . where space becomes sacred, hence pre-eminently *real.*"

For an embryo the center of the world is the navel—the point at which the umbilical cord brings nourishment from the mother's body. The ancient Greeks universalized this truth in the belief that Delphi, with its oracle, was the center (the navel or *omphalos*) of the world. For the ancient Jews, the Temple at Jerusalem was the sacred center of the world. These places were not merely geographical centers; they were central to, and symbols of, the meeting of the physical and spiritual dimensions of human experience.

For Christians, especially for those who celebrate liturgically, Jesus provides such a center in the sacrament of bread and wine. In order to see how this is so, we need to take a closer look at the words "sacrament" and "symbol." The Latin root *sacer* means "holy"; *ment* is a noun suffix denoting a means or resulting state. So a sacrament is a means to holiness. Now a look at the word "symbol." In ordinary usage a symbol stands for something that isn't there. In a more radical (root) sense, a sense in which some Greek Orthodox writers use it, a symbol is the very visibility of the invisible, the presence of the absent. Jesus' great gift of the sacrament of his body and blood, in the form of bread and wine, is the great symbol at the heart of the church.

A symbol in this high sense is a particular kind of emptying. H. Patrick Sullivan, an Anglican scholar, has said that the mystery of the Incarnation itself, the Word made flesh, is an emptying, a kenotic event (from Greek *kenoo*, to empty); that in Christ, God, without being depleted of divinity, "poured out" divinity into humanity: "I do not think it is stretching the theological meaning of *kenosis* to say that a symbol is a *kenotic* event, an 'emptying' of the sacred through its manifestations in perceptible form, a limitation of illimitable reality."

As Saint Paul wrote in his letter to the Colossians, "He is the image of the invisible God" (1:15). In that sense we may call Jesus the symbol of God. And as Jesus "empties" himself into bread and wine, *they* become symbols of Christ in this special sense: being absent from us he is also present with us.

The word "symbol" comes from two Greek roots: *sym* = with, together (as in symphony, to sound together) and *ballein* = to throw (as in ballistics). Christ's symbolic act of self-giving throws together the material and spiritual dimensions of our experience.

Jesus is both symbol and center. There are two kinds of movement around a center. The first is called centripetal. That's the kind of center a whirlpool has—a center that draws everything into itself. The second is called centrifugal—the center of an action which is like an electric mixer—which sends everything outward, sometimes spraying cake batter all over the counter! These two movements, drawing in and sending out, are central to human life. They are, first of all, the action of the heart—

systole and diastole; they are the action of our breath—breathing in and breathing out. Many things that may seem to be polarities may more truly be complementary.

Some communities and churches have put all their energy into one or the other of these movements, calling the drawing inward "liturgy" or "spirituality" and the sending outward "mission" or "apostolate." There can be real dissension about which to emphasize and put resources into. But as love must act, so there cannot be systole without diastole, or breathing in without breathing out. In our human bodies the heart draws in the blood and pumps it through the lungs to purify and renew it so that it may carry new life outward to the ends of our toes, and then it reverses the process. In the same way the life-renewing heart of God draws us into communion and nourishes us so that we may in turn go out into our communities— to the ends of the world—and give of what we have been given.

This gathering in and opening out is, in fact, the shape of the liturgy that we call Eucharist. It is the heart of the church. It is the reason for church. Many people think of the Eucharist, or Holy Communion, or the Mass, or the Lord's Supper, as it is variously called, as a service of words in a book. Historically, however, it is rather a series of actions: four actions, in fact—**take, bless, break, give.** "Then [Jesus] took a loaf of bread, and when he had given thanks, he broke it and gave it to them, saying, 'This is my body, which is given for you. Do this in remembrance of me.' And he did the same with the cup after supper, saying, 'This cup that is poured out for you is the new covenant in my blood'" (Luke 22:19-20).

This is the action of the Eucharist, and it consists first of a centripetal movement and then of a centrifugal. We draw together, we take or bring to the assembled company ourselves, our souls and bodies, time and talents, our gifts of bread, wine, and the money that symbolize our work; we bring our hopes, fears, and—as Saint Jerome learned—our sins. We offer all these things, blessing and giving thanks to God. So far it is an inward and upward movement. Jesus said, "And I, when I am lifted up from the earth, will draw all people to myself" (John 12:32). Then comes the breaking of the bread. In that breaking, all the brokenness of humanity is accepted and received into God, and through Jesus' broken body, transfigured with him. We are not only broken, but we are broken open, as a seed is broken open by the spring rains to send forth new life. With this opening the outward movement begins. Having taken, blessed, and broken, Jesus gave. We are given to and nourished so that we in turn may give to others. Jesus said, "Go into all the world and proclaim the good news to the whole creation" (Mark 16:15). Paul wrote to the church in Corinth, "Now you are the body of Christ and individually members of it" (1 Corinthians 12:27).

We are the body; we are the church. The rhythm of giving and receiving is not just the rhythm of the heart, the rhythm of breathing, it is the rhythm of love.

What about Prayer?

We often hear some version of a question like the following: "When the football players from both teams get down on their knees to pray before the game begins, how does God know which prayer to answer?" It might be a subtle poke at those who pray, disguised in the form of a rhetorical question; however, it does address the core issue of a significant debate: is there such a thing as a personal God who will individually look out for us and answer our particular questions, wishes, and dreams?

As so many people ask: "If there is a God, then why did my sister have to die?" "If there is a God who looks out for me, then why does my wife, who has faithfully gone to church, have cancer?" "If there is a God, why do most of the world's people suffer from poverty and disease while a handful enjoy wealth and prosperity?" "If there is a God, then why does it seem many of my prayers go unanswered?"

Thinking about the nature of God and of prayer is vital to our discussion here of filling the vessel. Because if we are not at all certain *how* or *if* the process of filling up with the Spirit works, then why empty? One potential barrier to inviting the Spirit is the difficulty of finding evidence that emptying and inviting the Spirit in is worth the risk.

One person said, "I am not a churchgoer, but I pray every single night. I have to admit though that there have been times when my prayers have not been answered. Once a friend's father was sick and I prayed for him to live. When he died, I was scared to death. If God won't answer a prayer as important as saving someone's life, then maybe we really are on our own here." When what we pray for doesn't happen, the inclination is to question God. It may be necessary to go through anger at God or a despairing kind of giving up. But eventually it is fruitful to come once again to the "If so, then what?" position. If we try to wait until we come to a place where we *can* see what's going on, keep hanging in with our truth and putting one foot in front of the other, we can come to where we can see and rejoice in how God is involved in our lives, even at the times when it feels least likely—even if it seems so many of our prayers go unanswered. .

Here is somewhat of an analogy—a parable, if you will—about the times when we don't see any markers or indicators of God's attention or action in our lives. The Eremo delle Carceri—the caves where Saint Francis and his brothers went to retreat and pray—are on Mount Subasio near Assisi, Italy. A three-mile hike up from the town, the road is fairly steep, consisting of a dry mustard-colored dirt that makes the shrubbery at its sides dusty and drab. There is no view. However, there are small turnouts by the roadside to rest and from there, between the foliage, the hiker can catch a glimpse of the bottom of the hill. After another consid-erable distance up the winding track, there is another turnout with a large rock on it—with an incredible view!

The whole valley around Assisi is spread beneath. There are olive orchards, fields being plowed by white oxen, the gate of the city and in the distance the great basilica of Santa Maria delle Angeli and a vista of hills and sky. Looking upward, the hiker catches a glimpse of the courtyard of the Eremo. It is thrilling! But if the hiker continues to sit in the sun, enjoy the breeze, and marvel at the vista, progress won't be made toward the top. In order to get where the hiker wants to go, he or she must forsake the splendid view and get back on that dusty, obscuring track of a road.

The real movement comes when the hiker slogs along seeing nothing much but dust! Thinking of this will help us wait for the larger perspec-tive and be patient about receiving any markers or indicators of God's involvement in our life. When there are no indications at all, that may in fact be just the time when real ground is being covered.

In the lonely stretches of dusty road when our level of trust in God's involvement in our life is very low, read the prayer that is called "Saint Teresa's Bookmark," which was found in Teresa's breviary at the time of her death in 1582:

> Nada te turbe,
> Nada te espante,
> Todo se pasa
> Dios no se muda,
> La paciencia
> Todo lo alcanza;
> Quien a Dios tiene
> Nada le falta;
> Solo Dios basta.

Which roughly translated is: "Let nothing disturb you, nothing frighten you: all things pass, only God remains. Patience gains everything, whoever has God needs nothing else; God alone is enough."

If there is a Creator God who created us in God's image as persons, then God must be at least as personal as we are. While God's divinity is beyond our comprehension, we can know God and have a personal relationship, not in the dimension of reason, but in love.

When Bad Things Happen

God somehow is personal to each of us and calls us to a love-relationship, which we call prayer. With that said, how do we explain when bad things happen to us? We have already talked about much that can contribute to some understanding of that problem, especially in chapters 6 and 7 when we were dealing with happiness and goodness and consequently with suffering and badness. The "five not-so-easy lessons from suffering to glory" with which we ended chapter 6 is one stab at understanding the purpose in bad things happening.

Another help is to remember playing cards as we did in chapter 6. A bad hand is a bad hand—but if everyone got a royal straight flush every time, there would be no game. If there had been no crucifixion, there would be no resurrection. We, too, must always try to learn more about what we are considering "bad" at each particular instance of diminishment.

Beginning to Pray

Prayer is a lifelong affair and in some sense there are no simple steps. It would be like talking about simple steps to begin a human love affair. In both cases, human and divine, we would try to make ourselves as attractive and wholesome as possible and think of what we have that we could give to our lover.

Beyond that, there are several areas in which to seek and meet God with **four** approaches to prayer. Even if a person began praying a long time ago, there is a need to begin again, the way we have to start each new day with waking. Saint Francis is reported to have said at the end of his life, "Brothers, let us begin again, for up to now we have done nothing."

1. **Nature.** Saint Thomas Aquinas said, "Grace builds on nature." Nature in this sense refers not only to fields of daffodils and sunsets but also to the complex reality in which we live. In cultural critic Morris Berman's book *The Reenchantment of the World,* he contends that, before Isaac Newton, the world was thought to be enchanted, full of wonder. Newtonian physics created the mind-set that, given time, humanity could measure and comprehend the entire natural world. Thus wonder and mystery gave way to knowledge.

This knowledge would give us more and more power to utilize and control the planet's resources, but also, unfortunately, the ability to exploit and diminish them. It is primarily the new sciences, particularly quantum physics, that have reopened the world to enchantment. We can no longer be certain that some day we will know it all, measure it all, control it all. Physicist Werner Heisenberg, for instance, asserted that we will never be certain of both the speed and the position of a given subatomic particle. When we admit uncertainty, we open the door to wonder, awe, and a reality greater than we can imagine.

This awareness is not, however, without antecedent. There were pioneers. Rudolf Otto published a book in 1917 called *Das Heilige,* translated as *The Idea of the Holy,* in which he used the word "numinous" to describe nature. In the 1940s and 1950s, the French Jesuit Teilhard de Chardin taught that all matter has a "within," thus confuting the popular polarization of the material and the spiritual. Now there are many people writing from this new, more integrated perspective. Some classics in this field are

Prayer: The Work of God

At our convent, the five times a day in chapel give a habitual shape to our life. The prayers we say at those times are in praise of God and they are focused around portions of the Psalter, or Psalms of David. Praying this way has traditionally been called the Opus Dei, the Work of God. People of the Covenants have been chanting these songs of praise since the days of the first great Temple in Jerusalem. The tones to which they were chanted in the Temple were the ones Saint Gregory the Great collected and standardized, and in the chapels of our convents we use an updated version of the Gregorian chant. From the times of the Desert Fathers and Mothers, the monastic life in the Christian tradition has always incorporated the saying of the psalms in a rotating cycle. I suppose one reason that chanting or reciting the psalms is so important to Christians is that they were, in a sense, Jesus' prayerbook; we hear in scripture that he quoted from them.

In addition to the daily Eucharist, we gather for the monastic "office" or round of prayer. These times in chapel provide us with a rhythm of praise: first thing in the morning, noontime, the end of the working day, and before bedtime. Somebody once called them the "escalator" of prayer. There I am, fretting a bit about letters to write, phone calls to make, travel plans to organize, meals to be served, people to talk to, or problems to be solved, and the bell rings for Vespers, the prayers at the end of the day's work. I drop everything else. The psalms, scripture readings, and hymns carry me up from the ground floor of my anxieties to a level of peace and praise. There is a good deal of silence before, during, and after these prayer times and the silence is as meaningful as the words. When I travel to do teaching or lead workshops, I sometimes miss that structure, but it is comforting to know that at home my Sisters are keeping it for me. When they are away on their various ministries and I am home, I likewise know I am singing God's praises for them.

—ES

Gary Zukov's *The Dancing Wu Li Masters*, K. C. Cole's *Sympathetic Vibrations*, Larry Dossey's *Time, Space and Medicine*, Thomas Berry's *The Dream of the Earth*, and Margaret Wheatley's *Leadership and the New Science*, to name only a few.

The point is that we are now being invited to see ourselves in a reenchanted world, where nature is a doorway into mystery—into the divine *mysterium tremendum*.

There are two things to watch out for as we approach God through nature. The first is to be aware of the difference between icon and idol. An icon is an image that invites participation in a reality beyond itself; an idol retains the meaning in itself. If we use nature as an idol we will never get beyond the sunset or the science to God. If we make ourselves or another person an idol, we will never see God in ourselves or in them. Hubert Northcott, an Anglican monk, wrote in *The Venture of Prayer*: "The sight and smell of a rose will come to one as a breath of heaven, drawing him [her] straight to worship. Another will be unable to get beyond its sensuous beauty and to that person it will be a hindrance."

The other thing to watch out for is the distinction between magic and miracle. *Magic* is always, in some way, an attempt to control or manipulate the physical and/or metaphysical world. *Miracle* is gift. The important question is not whether magic is intended for malevolent or benevolent effects, nor is it really whether magic works or not. It may "work." The borderland between the natural and supernatural orders is no doubt quite permeable, and we perhaps can sometimes or in some way predict or influence the way things happen.

But such attempts at control are at the opposite pole from the "dance" of spirit and Spirit. Again, the one is exploitation, the other gift. Think of an orange. The rind is edible, and if you were starving, it might provide some nourishment. In the same way it may be possible to nibble around the edges of the supernatural. But why bother? We are invited beyond the rind, beyond human attempts at control, into the juicy sweetness, the mystery of divine love!

2. Scripture. Unfortunately the Bible, also, can be made into an idol, and it's important to go beyond the written word to the Spirit of Truth who inspired the writers. Here's an analogy: think of the person who is dearest to you. Now suppose that person goes away—on a business trip, to school, or on a vacation. After a while you receive a letter or e-mail and what a wonderful message! Your person has written you about how much you mean to him or her, recalls special times you've shared, tells about some ways you have been especially helpful—all things that this person may have wanted to share with you but never said when with you. Well, you carry this letter or printout with you all day, and whenever you get a chance, you take it out of your pocket to be sure you've remembered exactly how this person described his or her love and gratitude for you and your relationship. When your day's work is done, you go to your favorite chair, put your feet up and take out your letter for a good, unhurried re-read. Just then the door opens—and surprise! Your person has unexpectedly returned! What do you do with your letter? You probably put it aside and go hug your dear one.

The Benedictine monks have a way of reading scripture that is very similar to this. It's called *lectio divina*. To practice this kind of scripture reading, read a passage only until you feel in the presence of the Living God, and then put down your Bible and rejoice in the presence of the Beloved.

3. In the depth of our being—or the height, or the ground. All dimensional descriptions for this meeting place are poetic—we might also call it the space in our being that has been emptied to receive the spirit. Though this "space" does not really have a "where" to it, we can sometimes think that below our conscious, subconscious, unconscious, there is a little trap door where, when it is opened, our individual spirit meets Holy Spirit. They meet, but *they do not merge.* Saint Bernard best describes this meeting:

> The union of God and man is brought about, not by confusion of natures, but by agreement of wills. Man and God, because they are not of one substance or nature, cannot be called "one thing," *unum* (like the father and the son); but they are in strict truth called "one spirit," if they adhere to one another by the glue of love.

If we *believe* this is true, we know God by faith, and that is what is important. If at rare moments we *experience* this meeting with God, that is what is called a mystical experience. It does not have to be like Saint Teresa in ecstasy. It can be a simple process like fretting over a problem for some time and then waking up the next morning with the answer in your head, clear as clear, and you don't know where it came from. That is an experience of the Holy Spirit of wisdom and truth communicating with your human spirit.

4. Other people. If God as Spirit is in me, then God is in you in the same way. This may sound easier to recognize than it is. Actually to see the compassion of God shine out of a pair of human eyes is quite rare. More often we see fear, defensiveness, protective mask, or ignorance— not compassion, but human frailty.

The people of India provide an interesting analogy. At one time in India people made lamps out of camel stomachs. When cured, these membranes had the consistency of parchment and the shape of globes. They were decorated with painted designs and then a candle was inserted at the bottom so that the globe served as a lampshade. Now the point is that the candle flame was the same in every lamp. But the shade varied greatly. Some camel stomachs were very thick and heavily decorated;

some were paper-thin and translucent. So with us human vessels. Even though the light is the same—for Christians, it is called the light of Christ—some shades, or personalities, are so thick and covered over, that it is almost impossible to *see* the light. Each of us has people in our lives with relatively thick shades. Equally, you can probably think of someone who for you seems to have a very thin shade, through whom you can see a good deal of light. This way of trying to know the truth of people is a wonderful way to approach God.

None of these ways, however, is a simple step. Maybe there are no simple steps; there is no owner's manual, because love cannot own, and love-objects cannot be owned. God knows we cannot find God easily in nature, in scripture, in the convolutions of our own hearts nor in those of others. So Jesus, quite simply, gives us his humanity and divinity in the consecrated bread and wine of the Eucharist. Granted, God is still hidden: "Truly you are a God who hides himself, O God of Israel, the Savior" (Isaiah 45:15). Hidden, yet in spirit met, and in love, known.

It is important to remember that prayer, like every other aspect of human life, is developmental. Many people seem to see prayer only as petitionary, "asking" prayer. That is: we ask, and God gives or doesn't give. That is only the beginning. It is natural for a baby, or any of us finding ourselves at a Level One (Levels of Love) point in our lives, to get into the "gimme, gimme" mode. But as we mature spiritually, so our spiritual relationship—prayer—becomes more mutual, and more like the dance analogy we introduced in chapter 2.

Here's another example. One day you meet a friend whom you've not seen for a couple of months. When you meet, your side of the dialogue runs roughly like this: "Hi! You look great! I like your hair that way. Listen, before we go have a cup of coffee, I need to say something. I know I promised to send you the title of that book we were talking about, but I totally forgot about it until this morning on the plane. I'm really sorry! What makes me feel worse is that *you* remembered to send me that article you found. It was very helpful to the research I was doing—thanks. Before I forget—I know you care a lot about my friend who is having a really rough time right now—more tests next week and the prognosis is not good. She's in my thoughts and prayers a lot; could you add your prayers? While we're on the subject—could you say a prayer for me too? I'm a little scared about going on that mission halfway round the world and working in such an unfamiliar culture. And could I borrow again your set of adapter plugs?"

It is because the friend's side of the dialogue, not recorded here, was so responsive that you feel free at the end to ask for a specific little thing that you need. In this somewhat typical conversation are five classical modes of prayer: adoration, contrition, thanksgiving, intercession, and petition! Everything in the conversation flows naturally out of the condition of a friendship. In the same way, your relationship to God is the ground and source of all the modes of your prayer. It's hard to ask something from a person from whom we feel distanced. However, if we feel close to somebody we feel free to ask just about anything. We trust the other to say no if they need to for any reason, and that a no will not in any way damage our relationship. Why shouldn't it be that way with God?

Relationship between Prayer and Emptiness

People who practice Zen meditation speak of acquiring "empty-mind." Also, Father Thomas Keating, co-founder of the modern contemplative prayer movement, uses an analogy of temptations and distractions in prayer being like little boats on a stream; the point is not to climb into them and get carried away, but just to recognize them and let them float by. Almost all of us need some sort of discipline to help us wake up, pay attention, and get beyond "busy-mind." The point is to make room for that welcoming space where our spirit meets with Holy Spirit. God's giving of God's self to us is an emptying of Godhead into humanity.

In a similar way, giving ourselves to God requires a self-emptying. As we've said, the thing about mature love is that it respects and makes room for the reality of the other as well as the reality of oneself. In our love-relationship with God, this is called prayer, and it requires a similar emptying of all the defenses and immature behaviors that might stand in the way of mutual self-gift.

How Should We Pray?

There is the discipline or practice of prayer, and the transcendence of the discipline. Brother Bede Thomas, O.H.C., used to say to his novices: "You think you have a prayer life? You don't have a prayer life, you just have life." That's one side of the paradox. The other side is that we *can* talk about a certain aspect of our lives, such as prayer. Prayer is a discipline, and is also beyond discipline.

A great deal of practice is needed in order to dance in a ballet or perform gymnastics so that these arts look effortless. Part of this training involves a routine—that is, a regular schedule of when and in what circumstances and how often to work at the skill. It's the same with prayer. The point is not the training; the point is the freedom and grace that the training eventually confers. When the discipline of prayer is transcended, when skill becomes art, *then* it begins to pervade one's whole life.

But before our "whole life is a prayer," we need to do some Olympic-class training. The practice of prayer almost always requires a consistency of time and place to begin with. Zen Buddhists know this well. If you ask a Zen teacher how to meditate, you will be told something like this: "Put your zafu (special pillow) on your zabuton (mat), sit in one of the classic (e.g. lotus or half-lotus) positions, straighten your spine, place your active hand under the other, thumbs touching lightly, rest your tongue lightly on the roof of your mouth, and focus your eyes on the ground about four feet in front of you. Now, count your breaths up to ten. When you can count up to ten without your mind wandering, practice watching your thoughts. Come back in a week." Alas! Christians don't have such a nicely ordered discipline, though many followers of Jesus adopt aspects of Zen practice for their own prayer.

At first we have to learn how to pay attention. Then we need to practice. One of the most helpful Christian disciplines of prayer we know comes from an Episcopal minister, the Very Reverend Alan Jones. He divides the time set aside for his meditation into three parts. That is, if he has half an hour, he divides it into three sections of ten minutes each; if he only has ten minutes total, then the divisions are roughly three periods of three minutes each. During the first section he pays attention to whatever is clamoring for his attention—no matter how un-edifying it is. He just lets the distraction or fantasy have its day. Then in the second part of his time he invites God into the picture, to look alongside him at what he is so caught up in, and tries to see it with God's "eyes" or perspective. (This of course isn't helpful if one's God is a judgmental God but only if God is an ally who can bring compassion, and possibly humor, to the situation.) Then in the third period of time, having paid attention and due respect to whatever is going on for him, there is the possibility of simply being still and present with God.

This isn't so far from the Buddhist practice of watching your thoughts. The point is that forcibly suppressing distractions won't work, but if you let them play themselves out in a fairly ordered time frame they may eventually run themselves down. At that point you can in effect say to them, "Okay, we've run this scenario through a number of times—your turn may come again, but for now, why don't you go for a while and let me be quiet?"

Again, a discipline of prayer usually needs to start with a routine, a sameness of time and place. Perhaps a place that already is, or we have made, sacred space by keeping silence there and some icon of God's love. Eventually special times and places of prayer will spread out into our lives, so that in a sense one's whole life is a prayer. However, it is still as important to have quality time with the divine lover as it is with human lovers.

It is a question of attention, practice, and joyful giving of oneself to the partner and the "music" in the "dance" of prayer. If we are loving a human being with a Level One Love, the chances are that our love will be immature and narcissistic. To stretch the dance metaphor, we will be trying to pull our partner around and even if we force our partner to go in the direction we want to go some of the time, the main outcome will be frustration and stepping on each other's feet. The analogy holds fairly true with Levels Two and Three. We need to ripen in prayer, just as we do physically and psychologically. Growth in each dimension informs the others.

Expectations of Prayer

The most common mistake that people make when they pray has to do with expectations. People tend, knowingly or unknowingly, to come to their prayer time or retreat time with certain preconceptions about what they should or could feel during prayer. It may be helpful to name these possible feelings and then try to empty ourselves of expecting any or all of them.

First, there are "the pits." If we stop doing and are quiet, we might become aware of things better left *un-thought*. Memories might escape from

Learning the Intimacy of Prayer

Sometimes our maturing in prayer happens imperceptibly, but once in a while it is noticeable. One of those "quantum leaps" happened to me at a time decades ago when I was handling two jobs, either of which alone would have challenged me. Under this pressure I felt myself at times regressing back to my self-image of the needy orphan waif. One evening I was in my office after a long day of being pressed for time and picked at and projected on by the people with whom I lived and worked. I was frazzled. I realized that in the office next to mine my Superior was also working late. She was a woman of great wisdom and compassion. It occurred to the orphan waif in me to run to her, unload my neediness, and ask for sympathy and affirmation. Then another voice within me posed the question: What would it be like not to do that? She, too, has had a long day and is surely trying to wind up her affairs so she can get to bed. What if you spared her and took all this directly to God? And so I went into the chapel. I was just at the point of unloading all my neediness onto God, when a question once more posed itself within me— What if I didn't dump it all on God either?

It seemed a very clear invitation. I found in that instant that I could accept—that I could choose not to throw myself helplessly on the other— even God. That I could contain my spirit and simply be there. What followed was indescribable, but I'll attempt a few words anyway. It was a moment of the most unbelievable intimacy between my spirit and Holy Spirit—of a free exchange, of myself simply present to God and God to me. My Level One neediness, instead of being ministered to, was elevated to a Level Three mutual gift. I understood in a new way Jesus' saying: "I do not call you servants any longer . . . but I have called you friends" (John 15:15).

—ES

our unconscious that we have shoved down there because they were too awful. We might find out how angry we are or how sad, or remember some horrible thing we did to someone or that had been done to us. Or we might discover that we really don't believe there is any meaning to life or any God or that anyone cares that we are on earth or not. Saint Paul's words are a sort of talisman for such times and can be a real comfort to cling to: "For I am convinced that neither death, nor life, nor angels, nor rulers, nor things present, nor things to come, nor powers, nor height, nor depth, nor anything else in all creation, will be able to separate us from the love of God in Christ Jesus our Lord" (Romans 8:38-39).

So then we can tell our dreadful thoughts to go sit on the shelf for a while.

The second expectation might be that prayer will be, even if not horrendous, still repulsive. We won't like sitting there. Why should we put ourselves through this frustration?

The third expectation is that even if it isn't distasteful, it will be simply boring, a waste of time, when we have so many more productive things to do.

The fourth expectation is that it will be at least relaxing. We will just be quiet, and all our worries and tiredness will drop away.

The fifth expectation is that prayer will be a time of illumination. All sorts of things will become clear to us—and the Spirit will inspire us with brilliant truths and beautiful thoughts.

The sixth expectation is that our prayer should be union with God—a sense of God's presence and a kind of basking in it.

Now the mistake in hanging on to these expectations is that any one of them or all of them or something entirely different might happen. Or might not. Have you ever been looking forward to seeing a friend (or an adversary) and find yourself imagining a conversation with them? It hardly ever turns out the way you expect. If we empty ourselves of expectations, a conversation with our friend may take surprisingly delightful turns, and one with our adversary might be blessed with a step toward reconciliation. As Woody Allen is quoted as saying: "Eighty-five percent of life is showing up." So, too, in our conversation with God. Just show up, and anything can happen. It's all part of the relationship.

The expectation we call "illumination" needs a little more explanation. Sometimes people make a mistake in thinking an illumination, or light bulb thought, comes from God when it really doesn't. If there's any doubt where a special idea or vision came from, that's a good time to go to someone who has been saying their prayers a long time and whom you trust, or who is recommended to you as a trustworthy person in spiritual matters. It's easy to make the mistake that a thought came from the Holy Spirit of truth, when, in fact, it came from another spirit entirely.

Saint Teresa of Avila had some solid teaching about this discernment. Roughly, she said that a thought or vision is from the spirit of truth if it: (1) brings with it peace and harmony—not unease—and leaves you refreshed and not exhausted, (2) if it cannot easily be forgotten, and (3) if there is an intuitive sense that you did not compose the experience yourself. When the thought or vision comes from the spirit of lies, or one's own spirit alone, it may: (1) be disturbing and disquieting, and there may be agitation during the time that it lasts; (2) it may produce darkness and affliction in the soul; and (3) it may leave you with dryness and disinclination toward prayer and good works.

Basically, if after any such illumination, we feel cheered, renewed, and peacefully energetic, and if we feel grateful for a gift that has brought us closer to God, then we *have* received such a gift. They are called consolations. Very often they are "honeymoon" gifts, so as the spiritual relationship matures, they may fall away. Not to worry. Remember the quote from Saint Paul's letter to the Romans: nothing can separate us from the love of God. If, however, you feel more anxious, compelled to act in a certain direction, or distraught, then it may be not an illumination from the Holy Spirit, but a smoke screen from the spirit of untruth. Best then to check it out.

And just a word about telling people about your consolations in prayer. Checking them out with a wise person like a spiritual director is one thing—and a very good thing. But telling all and sundry is questionable. Before you do, ask yourself what you're doing it for. We can use the analogy of speaking of the intimacies of a human love. Often it doesn't really edify the one to whom it is told, but either bores them or makes them jealous.

Another mistake people often make around expectations in prayer is not in the area of feelings but of results. We should try to empty ourselves of the expectation of seeing any results at all—even of "growing" or getting somewhere in our prayer life. That's really the point of the story about climbing Mount Subasio. Just try to show up, choose reality, and keep going.

Prayer Releases God within Us

We have discussed various ideas.

There is the thought of the soul having the capacity for infinite reality to be held finitely. There is Saint Bernard's description of human spirit meeting Holy Spirit. There is also Saint Paul's, "Do you not know that you are God's temple and that God's Spirit dwells in you?" (1 Corinthians 3:16). And, Teilhard's contention that there is no dichotomy of matter and spirit—that all matter has a "within." God's Spirit *is* within us, greets our spirit, and releases in us an abundance of divine energy. The first and last thing we can say about God in us and us in God is that, being a love relationship, it is as inexplicable as the existence of love itself.

We are called to grow in love, choose the truth, and risk all for joy, that we "may become participants of the divine nature" (2 Peter 1:4). This could be the call of the Divine Lover:

> Where have you peace?
> Thoughts will not cease;
> dreams give you no release
>
> Sense is a snare;
> all things a care—
> time but a comet's flare.
>
> Put not your trust
> in things of dust;
> fame's but a mumbled crust.
>
> I am the bread;
> take me instead,
> all without me is dead.
>
> Would you be free?
> Love, look at me—
> I am eternity.

CHAPTER TEN

Vessel of Peace

As we approached the end of writing the book, we felt as though we needed to conclude with a discussion of the essence of the teachings we have been exploring—the core message that we can take with us as we attempt to move toward becoming vessels for peace. Write the key phrases and keep them near—or better, memorize to have them with you daily.

- **Move toward Unconditional Acceptance.** We are unconditionally loved, and the goal of spiritual growth is to move toward living and loving unconditionally.

- **Practice Emptiness Every Day.** In order to fill up with unconditional love, we need to be vigilant in emptying ourselves of all that which is not unconditional love.

- **Act from One's Own Center.** This is the notion that God's will for us is identical to our deepest desire. Therefore, we must constantly look for and stay aligned with that deepest desire.

- **Choose the Good.** Since we have been given free will and the power to choose both good and evil, living as a vessel of peace means choosing that which is good, that which fosters love and acceptance.

Move toward Unconditional Acceptance

Perhaps the most important foundational idea is that we are unconditionally loved and accepted as creatures of God. It is truly remarkable how many people seem to live their lives in constant negotiation with what they see as a judgmental God. There is tremendous power in the idea that irrespective of what we do, we are unconditionally accepted exactly the way we are. The reason so many of us have trouble believing this idea is because we fail to see the difference between divine *unconditional* acceptance and human *conditional* acceptance. And even those of us who see this distinction spend so much more of our time in the realm of the human, with its rigid conditions and judgment, that divine unconditionality has little or no chance to take hold.

Many of the myths that we have explored are purely human constructions, beliefs that have emerged through millennia between and among human beings. The hope for humanity lies in more of us emptying ourselves of the pathology of these myths in order to drink in the unconditional acceptance available in the space between myths, in emptiness. Too often, we become filled with human nonacceptance to the exclusion of divine acceptance. To the extent that we become attached to these human judgments and worry about our place in the human world, it is easy to forget God's fundamental acceptance of us.

The realization of divine unconditional acceptance will fundamentally change the way we are in the world. How do we become convinced that we are unconditionally accepted by God, even if not by our fellow humans? By listening to the wisdom of important others and from our own reflections, logical reasoning, and study of the wisdom literature, not the least of which is the Bible itself:

> He said to his disciples, "Therefore I tell you, do not worry about your life, what you will eat, or about your body, what you will wear. For life is more than food, and the body more than clothing. Consider the ravens: they neither sow nor reap, they have neither storehouse nor barn, and yet God feeds them. Of how much more value are you than the birds! And can any of you by worrying add a single hour to your span of life? If then you are not able to do so small a thing as that, why do you worry about the rest? Consider the lilies, how they grow: they neither toil nor spin; yet I tell you, even Solomon in all his glory was not clothed like one of these". (Luke 12:22-27)

We are unconditionally loved and accepted by God—God IS love. To the extent that we embody love and acceptance for ourselves and for others, we are the embodiment of God and/or spirit. We are, in short, vessels for love. "There is no fear in love, but perfect love casts out fear" (1 John 4:18). If God unconditionally loves us, then what is there to be afraid of?

In our lives, fears are based on not understanding the scope of the gift we have been given. If we are so busy doing things to gain human love or approval, we can't come to understand love. But the lilies of the field do not worry what the trees in the adjacent forest think of them. Indeed, one branch of the tree doesn't worry what another branch thinks of it. Perhaps we should stop worrying what others think of us. Whenever we seem to be drifting away from the sense of divine unconditional love, we should try to focus on Jesus' image of the lilies blowing in the fields, soaking in the sunshine, free from fear, free from the human stresses we experience.

A great Eastern sage, Sri Nisargadatta, when asked if only saints had unconditional love, said that everyone has unconditional love; the difference is most of us have other things that get in the way. Perhaps the challenge of embodying spirit and becoming a vessel for peace is to become more and more filled with unconditional love and less filled with judgment and hatred.

Practice Emptiness Every Day

The concept of emptiness is an essential teaching of this book. We are constantly exposed to messages that have the effect of filling up our vessels. The task is to continually seek ways to empty oneself of the cultural noise that gets in the way of spiritual growth. If we do not make intentional efforts to empty, there will be no room for the spirit of peace to enter. Robert Morneau likens it to having no room at the inn:

> On their travels, tourists seeking accommodations watch for the "Vacancy" sign outside motels. Dismay sets in when, one after the other, all they see is the cruel "No Vacancy" message which happy proprietors switch on when every room is filled. This image reflects when life is cluttered with excessive activity, glutted with material possession . . . It can well happen that the consumption of time and energy is so great that the mystery of God is shelved, if not forgotten. There is simply no inner space and the divine Guest remains at the door, facing the blinking "No Vacancy" sign. Matters of the spirit are thus ignored or neglected.

It is vital that we consistently take steps to empty out such barriers to the divine spirit. We've mentioned some strategies for prayer that can help. Also, establishing regular times for contemplation and meditation is useful to regain a sense of perspective on one's purpose and role in this fast-moving society.

The key to emptying is self-awareness. We cannot empty that which we are not aware of. Self-awareness has entered the mainstream of intellectual thought as even corporations begin to understand the importance to their success of finding and keeping employees who have high levels of what can be termed "emotional intelligence"—the ability to manage one's own emotional states and to understand those of others. Only by looking inward at the forces that fill us up and stress us out can we begin to learn how to manage those forces and move toward peace.

Act from One's Own Center

The key to spiritual growth is to move away from following the "thou shalts" that society thrusts upon us and to become a person who is acting from one's own center. To get to this point, we must fully embrace the other key learnings described thus far—in order to muster the strength to follow our own path, we must be convinced that it is the will of God for us to do so.

And while the call is to follow our deepest desires, there is scant evidence of this truth in our culture. Everywhere we turn, we are encouraged not to follow our own deepest desires but rather to follow the deepest desires of those others in the marketplace who want us to buy something from them and, in effect, follow their lead.

It is in many ways the ultimate act of courage to follow one's own deepest yearnings. There are strategies one can employ to make the transition easier, such as finding a guide, joining a group of others who are trying to make a similar transition, and inviting the spirit to join you along the way. The goal is to be a more inner-directed, intentional person who seeks his or her own deepest desires and follows them in concert with the Spirit. In short, it is about finding peace, and the best way to promote peace on earth is to start with oneself. By emptying our individual vessels of the surface chatter of cultural myths and judgment, most of which are merely artificial human constructs, we make room for the flow of eternal love and peace that, like the ancient rivers, flows freely and naturally.

Choose the Good

A major idea that we have described in this book builds on the others. A primary truth is that we are unconditionally accepted and consequently are free to do whatever we choose to do. What this means is that how and what we choose becomes of paramount importance. For while we may be guaranteed freedom, we are not guaranteed wholeness or fulfillment. As we wrote in chapter 1, we will get *old* just by breathing, but we may not necessarily get *ripe*.

Becoming ripe and whole is a byproduct of choosing that which is good *over the long term*, and this requires hard work, reflection, and intentionality. We were given a most precious gift, the gift of free will. But with such a gift comes tremendous responsibility.

In religious circles, much is made of the process of discernment. This is really just another word for thinking about a decision before making it. The two areas to think about are *how* to choose and *what* to choose.

With regard to the how, one of the most powerful strategies that can improve our choice-making ability is to think about the empty space or gap between stimulus and response. When we experience a stimulus during the day, a particularly stressful interaction with a boss or a negative comment from a coworker or a car cutting us off on the freeway, we can use these events as signals to stop and reflect on the events, rather than just reacting impulsively. The idea is to think about our emotional state right after the event and to think about all of the things that led up to the person reacting the way he or she did. Then, before taking action, ask the "what" question: "What can I choose that will foster good news in the long run?" Joy and peace are manifestations of choosing the good.

The longer and more consistently we can live in the gap or emptiness, the easier it becomes to really evaluate the full range of options before acting. Think of these moments as "God moments" because they are opportunities for us to incorporate God's unconditional love into our daily lives. It is in this gap or empty space between stimulus and response that one can tap into unconditional love and find compassion. The mystics call it the dwelling place of God. The longer we can evaluate a situation, living in the gap, the more compassion we can find building up inside us. It is almost like pulling off the road and stopping to fill up with gas. We stop to fill up with compassion. But if we go too long without stopping, we'll run out. The goal should be to evolve to the point where we can regularly step into the gap and fill up our tanks with compassion in order to become, as Saint Francis says, an instrument of God's peace.

The essence of the teaching in this book is consciousness. The glory, and the challenge, of our nature as *Homo sapiens* is to become more and more aware. When God asked the young Solomon what he desired above all things, Solomon chose wisdom, or an understanding and discerning mind (1 Kings 3:5-12). Consciousness develops, or ripens, along with the other aspects of our lives. These come as an invitation or call; as with any call, each can be responded to, ignored, or actively resisted.

First there is the call to **wake up**. This is the point at which a person sees *what is*, not what one expects to see, or has been taught to see. It is the day when we ask, "Is this all there is?"

Second, after the wakening there is the call to **choose the truth,** to make a commitment to reality. Often this is a very difficult thing to do, and it reminds us of the passage in Genesis 32:24-30 in which Jacob wrestles all night with the angel of God. Though he is wounded, he prevails at dawn, and receives a blessing and a new name. Finding our truth in God's reality often comes only after a long time in the dark and a hard wrestling match, but the prize for "persistence" and maybe suffering some pain is a new sense of being.

Third, there is the call to **see the larger picture**—or a more comprehensive perspective. In a museum we can walk into a gallery and on the far wall see a landscape by Van Gogh. We are struck with the power and beauty of the overall design. At that distance it is by far the most arresting picture in the room, but slowly as we move closer, within a foot of the canvas, we see not the whole structure but the unique contribution of each marvelous brushstroke. We can't see both the whole design and each brushstroke at the same time, but the problem is with the limitation of our vision and not with the painting. So also with our comprehension of reality. Even though we cannot see the whole picture while we are conscious of a moment's "brushstroke," there is the call mentally and spiritually to "stand back," to try to place the awareness of the particular moment in the context of eternity.

And finally there is the call to **grow in love**. The point here is to try to remember what we are growing in awareness *of*. Cosmic, divine reality—God—is Love. It is not enough merely to become aware—there must be an action toward Love. We can grow in love toward ourselves—becoming aware that at any given moment our best is good enough—in fact, it is wonderful—so long as we grow in conscious discernment of how to choose the best. We can grow in love toward others. Their best is their best. Our constant question should be, how can we relate to them in a way that nurtures their growth in awareness of the good? And, there is always the call to grow in love with the consciousness and trust of knowing God's love.

Pouring the myths, the lies, the unwanted from the vessel requires a firm hand. Practicing emptiness to obtain peace is not about giving up all of our worldly possessions and sitting under a Bo tree, nor is it about running off to a monastery and praying eight hours a day. It is very much about making the world our own monastery and walking through it with a true sense of connection to oneself, to others, and to God. It is filling to overflowing our vessel with peace.

SECTION 3
Notes

Key Terms

Attachment—Attachment is the psychological glue that connects us to beliefs and myths. The literal definition comes from the French "attaché" meaning to "nail to." Thus to attach oneself to something is to literally become nailed to it. Attachment is a primary source of stress and anxiety when we become "nailed to" cultural lies.

A central idea in the Zen tradition is to practice watching one's thoughts and then let them go by. The thoughts are driven by beliefs that are part of an overall mythology to which we so often attach ourselves. The process of emptying out is the process of detaching from these myths and beliefs: paying attention to them, observing them, even feeling them, but then letting them go along their way to make room for the next thing. A key message in *Vessel of Peace* is that to get the most out of life, one must accept things the way they are, experience them fully, but then let them go on their way. We are creatures who tend to either run away from things or attach ourselves to them and consequently get stuck. In many ways, this book is about how to run full steam into life without getting stuck.

Belief—Belief is a state or habit of mind in which trust or confidence is placed in some person or thing. We are using the word to mean the "habits of mind" that get installed into our consciousness by family, peer groups, and the culture and, when taken together, comprise the myth discussed. Beliefs are the sort of psychological software that, consciously or unconsciously, drive our thinking and behavior. Some of these beliefs can "fill up" our psyche and cause enormous stress. For example, you might internalize the belief that you can someday write the perfect book and so this belief becomes a component part of the overall cultural myth of perfection described in chapter 1.

Community-Building—At times we refer to "community-building." It is a three-day retreat model that was originally created by M. Scott Peck and a group of people who ran The Foundation for Community Encouragement from 1985 to 2000. This workshop-type model brings a group of people together to give them the opportunity to empty themselves of that which is getting in the way of finding their true purpose and to explore their relationships with others and with God. For a complete description of the community-building workshop process, see M. Scott Peck, *The Different Drum: Community Making and Peace* (New York: Simon and Schuster, 1987) and Doug Shadel and Bill Thatcher, *The Power of Acceptance: Building Meaningful Relationships in a Judgmental World* (Los Angeles: Newcastle Publishing, 1997).

Myth—Of the classical myths it has been said, "History is the vehicle for fact; myth is the vehicle for truth." A traditional meaning of "myth" is something that happened once but also happens all the time. While classical myths like the Myth of Sisyphus are vehicles for truth, there are many "cultural" myths that are, in effect, vehicles for untruth or lie. It is these "cultural lies" that we address as myths. They are cultural phenomena that are true to the extent they exist and are present in the culture, but false in terms of what they point toward: namely a reality that brings meaning and fulfillment to one's life. In consumer protection terms, we would call these myths a kind of "bait and switch" in which we are led to believe that if we do "A" then "B" will follow: if you just follow the myth of perfection, you will find satisfaction; if you buy into the myth that you can control your environment totally, then you will feel fulfilled; if you accumulate enough material possessions, you will be happy, and so on.

Spiritual Director or Guide—A spiritual director is someone who accompanies individuals as they explore a deeper relationship with the spiritual aspect of being human. One important characteristic to look for in a spiritual director is a maturity in spirituality that can enable the director to bracket his or her own agenda and emotions while he or she is there for the other. Selecting someone for a spiritual guide can be difficult because it is such a personal interaction and because there are many thousands of spiritual directors who never advertise their services. In terms of what kind of person to look for, our general advice is to select someone who has been saying their prayers for a couple of decades and whose opinion you trust in other areas. In order to find such a person, we suggest you start by asking trusted leaders in your faith community for a referral to someone who may do spiritual direction. In addition, there are a number of websites that offer excellent, objective information about spiritual direction from a variety of religious perspectives. While we do not endorse any particular website, an example of such a site is Spiritual Directors International (www.sdiworld.org).

Credits

Chapter 1: The Myth of Perfection

Alice Miller, *For Your Own Good: Hidden Cruelty in Child-Rearing and the Roots of Violence* (New York: Noonday Press, 1990).

M. Scott Peck, *The Road Less Traveled: A New Psychology of Love, Traditional Values and Spiritual Growth* (New York: Simon and Schuster, 1978).

Mother, Paramount Pictures, 1996.

Chapter 2: The Myth of Control

W. F. Adams, S.S.J.E. and Gilbert Shaw, *Triumphant in Suffering: A Study in Reparation* (London: Mowbray, 1951).

Chapter 3: The Myth of Accumulation

Frederick Buechner, *Wishful Thinking: A Seeker's ABC* (New York: Harper Collins, 1993).

Joe Dominquez and Vicki Robin, *Your Money or Your Life* (London: Penguin Books, 1993).

Lewis Hyde, *The Gift: Imagination and The Erotic Life of Property* (New York: Vintage Books, 1983).

Martha Rogers and Don Peppers, *The One to One Future* (New York: Doubleday Press, 1993).

Robert J. Spitzer, *The Spirit of Leadership: Optimizing Creativity and Change in Organizations* (Provo, Utah: Executive Excellence Publishing, 2000).

Thorstein Veblen, *The Theory of the Leisure Class* (Mineola: Dover Thrift Edition, 1994).

Chapter 4: The Myth of Limitlessness
Wayne Dyer, *The Sky's the Limit* (New York: Simon and Schuster, 1981).
Parker Palmer, *Let Your Life Speak* (San Francisco: Jossey Bass, 2000).
M. Scott Peck, The *Road Less Traveled and Beyond: Spiritual Growth in An Age of Anxiety* (New York: Simon and Schuster, 1997).
Juliet B. Schor, *The Overspent American: Upscaling, Downshifting, and the New Consumer* (New York: Basic Books, 1998).

Chapter 5: The Myth of Individualism
Martin Buber, *I and Thou* (New York: Touchstone, 1996).
Irving Yalom, *The Theory and Practice of Group Psychotherapy* (New York: Basic Books, 1977).

Chapter 6: The Myth of Happiness
Joseph Campbell and Bill Moyers, *The Power of Myth* (New York: Anchor, 1991).
Stephanie Coontz, *The Way We Never Were* (New York: Basic Books, 1992).
T. S. Eliot, *Murder in the Cathedral* (London: Faber and Faber Limited, 1952).
Carl Jung in Anthony Storr, *The Essential Jung* (Princeton: Princeton University Press, 1983).
American Beauty, Dreamworks Pictures, 2000.

Chapter 7: The Myth of Being Good
Anthony Bloom, *Beginning to Pray* (Mahwah: Paulist Press, 1982).
C. S. Lewis, *Mere Christianity* (New York: Harper Collins, 1996).
Martin Seligman, *Learned Optimism: How to Change Your Mind and Your Life* (New York: Vintage Books, 2006).

Chapter 8: Transition
Margie Lachman and Jacqueline Boone James, *Multiple Paths of Midlife Development: The John D. and Catherine T. MacArthur Foundation Series on Mental Health* (Chicago: University of Chicago Press, 1997).
C. S. Lewis, *Mere Christianity* (New York: Harper Collins, 1996).

Chapter 9: Filling Up with the Spirit

Saint Bernard, Sermon LXXI, on the Song of Songs in Dom Cuthbert Butler, *Western Mysticism* (London: Constable Publishers, 1926).

Morris Berman, *The Reenchantment of the World* (Cornell: Cornell University Press, 1981).

Mircea Eliade, *The Sacred and the Profane* (New York: Harcourt, 1959).

Hubert Northcott, C. R., *The Venture of Prayer* (London: SPCK, 1954).

H. Patrick Sullivan, "Ritual: Attending to the World," *Anglican Theological Review*, Supplementary Series #5, June 1975.

Leap of Faith, Paramount Pictures, 1992.

Chapter 10: Vessel of Peace

Robert Morneau, *Spiritual Direction: Principles and Practices* (New York: The Crossroads Company, 1992).

About the Authors

Ellen Stephen (ES) is an Episcopalian nun of the Order of Saint Helena and has served in leadership in her community for many years. She conducts Quiet Days and Retreats and is a spiritual director at the convent where she lives in the mid-Hudson Valley of New York state. ES travels widely as a facilitator and consultant on community and spirituality.

Doug Shadel is a longtime advocate for consumers and older persons and currently serves as the state director of AARP Washington. He has cowritten several books, including *The Power of Acceptance: Building Meaningful Relationships in a Judgmental World* and *Weapons of Fraud: A Sourcebook for Fraud Fighters*. He has a Ph.D. in social psychology and lives in Seattle with Renee, his wife, and son and daughter, Nick and Emily.